FROM DISCONTENT

FROM DISCONTENT

The Biography of a Mystic

by

Bruce Wells

GEORGE RONALD
OXFORD

GEORGE RONALD, Publisher
46 High Street, Kidlington, Oxford, OX5 2DN

ISBN 0–85398–206–6 (hardcover)
ISBN 0–85398–207–4 (softcover)

Typeset by Sunrise Setting,
Torquay, Devon
Printed in England

CONTENTS

BOOK II: YOUTH
Being the next six years of Adam's life

ILLUSTRATIONS

Author's Dedication

This book is dedicated to youth of high ambition and to all those who are traveling in their own way along this path. I hope that each finds a little of himself in the mystic and a little of the Mystic in himself.

Adam's Dedication

To each of the Persian believers who asked, 'How did you become a Bahá'í?'

ACKNOWLEDGEMENTS

That you are reading this book is due to the work of many more people than just its author. Of these four should be named. I wish to thank E.P. Menon and Marion Hofman for their open-handed, open-hearted encouragement; Steven Scholl for suggesting the twists; and May Ballerio, the editor, for bringing the project to completion. I am indebted to Paul Simon and Charing Cross Music, Inc, 114 East 55th St., New York, for permission to quote 'The Boxer'; Jim Seals and Dash Crofts, and Dawnbreaker Music Inc, 1230 Avenue of the Americas, New York, for 'East of Ginger Trees'; the heirs of John Lennon, Paul McCartney, and Northern Songs Ltd, 19 Upper Brook Street, London, for 'Come Together'. I also wish to thank W.W. Norton and Co. for the quotation from Ortega y Gasset's *Meditations on Quixote*, translated by Evelyn Rugg and Diego Marín; and all those who have allowed me to use paintings and drawings in their possession as illustrations for this book. Full acknowledgement of these is given on the relevant pages.

How is it possible for that which does not exist – a projected adventure – to govern and alter harsh reality? Perhaps it is not possible, but it is a fact that there are men who decide not to be satisfied with reality. Such men aim at altering the course of things; they refuse to repeat gestures that custom, tradition or biological instincts force them to make. These men we call heroes, because to be a hero means to be one out of many, to be oneself. If we refuse to have our actions determined by heredity or environment, it is because we seek to base the origins of our actions on ourselves and only on ourselves. The hero's will is not that of his ancestors nor of his society, but his own. This will to be oneself is heroism.

Ortega y Gasset, *Meditations on Quixote*

FOREWORD

Being the author's apology

Two aspects of this book need an explanation. The first is the use of the story of Joseph from the Old Testament. I chose it to parallel Adam's story, that each might mirror and shed more light on the other. The story of Joseph is presented in such a way as to make this use of it clear.

The story of Joseph is both ancient and great. It has become a shared inheritance of the religions of the Semitic branch: the Jewish, the Christian, the Islamic, the Bábí and the Bahá'í. Its universality lends to it various interpretations. Perhaps the most weighty of these paints Joseph as the Manifestation of God. I, however, have chosen to concentrate on Joseph as the eternal seeker rather than the One sought because this book is the biography of a beginning – and only that.

Be all that as it may, Adam insists that I quote the Hoopoe's reply to the Sparrow: 'O you, who in your despondency are sometimes sad, sometimes gay, I am not deceived by these artful pleas. You are a little hypocrite. Even in your humility you show a hundred signs of vanity and pride. Not another word, sew up your lips and put your foot forward. If you burn, you will burn with the others. And don't compare yourself with Joseph' (Attar, *The Conference of the Birds*, trans. C. S. Nott).

The second aspect of this book which bears comment is the story of Adam himself. The story is true, but only in essence. It is, more or less, my autobiography; although it was written to be read as something more than that. Personal and geographical names have been changed or rearranged. There are two reasons for this: the first is that I could never remember names correctly; the second is that should anyone recognize himself but feel my portrait to be unjust, a way is left open to deny it. On the other hand, should anyone who knows say that any particular part of the story did not happen, believe them; they are probably right. But that does not make the story any less true.

My story-teller is a woman (perhaps my *anima* image) who, for the time being – the book is about the progress of her development just as much as it is of mine – recommends herself to my imagination as Rebecca Abrams. I have chosen the female narrator, in tribute to Rebecca, because my life has been unfailingly influenced and guided by women and by the feminine principle, both positively and negatively, both by their presence and by their absence. Nonetheless, the book was written by a man about a man. Let this serve to explain any inner inconsistency of attitude regarding the relationship and revolution of the sexes. These inconsistencies exist (I seem to progressively understand less and less about 'Woman', just as I progressively understand less and less about 'God' – *Das Unbeschreibliche, / Hier ist's getan; / Das Ewigweibliche, / Zieht uns hinan*)* and although they may detract from the 'art' of the book, I believe that inconsistency is an ultimate essential of our nature, whereas minor consistencies can never hope or aspire to be.

I hope you enjoy and are uplifted by the story I set before you.

December 1983.

* Goethe, *Faust, Part Two*; concluding lines: 'Here the ineffable / Wins life through love; / Eternal Womanhood / Leads us above.' Trans. Philip Wayne.

PROLOGUE

Being where the author describes her first meeting with Adam

I first spoke with Adam in a small back street cafe off Ghandi Marg
in New Delhi. I was in India trying to escape the rush and push of
the modern West and I think, in part, he was doing the same thing.
In fact, I think that most of us who have found ourselves in India
have gone there to escape something or to find something (and the
two are not so different as they might seem).

I was feeling lonely that evening and, since he was sitting alone
having tea and looked relatively harmless, I asked if I might sit with
him. He later told me that he would have been much too shy to ask
the same thing! We talked about how we each happened to be in
India, about ourselves and our interests. It is surprisingly easy to
escape the trivialities of conversation when you are thousands of
miles away from home.

As was perhaps inevitable, there were many things similar in our
lives, although there were also many things vastly different. It may
be because of the similarities that it first occurred to me to write this
story. It was our mutual interest in writing that confirmed our
relationship – he was a poet and I enjoyed writing short stories and
thought of dabbling with a novel. We were both full of hope.

We spent the better part of that night talking, and we both went
away well satisfied with the evening. We kept fairly close company
those first two months in Delhi and have continued to meet since
then, both in India, and here at home, whenever circumstances have
permitted. We have spoken long and often – usually midnight
conversations by candlelight, moonlight or the light from paper
lanterns in small cafes – and it was from these conversations that this
story grew.

I hope that from this story you come to love Adam as I have.

Book I
CHILDHOOD
Being the first eighteen years of Adam's life

Better is a poor and a wise child than an old and foolish king, who will no more be admonished. For out of prison he cometh to reign; whereas also he that is born in his kingdom becometh poor. I considered all the living which walk under the sun, with the second child that shall stand up in his stead. There is no end of all the people, even of all that have been before them: they also that come after shall not rejoice in him. Surely this also is vanity and vexation of spirit.

Ecclesiastes 4:13–16

When I left my home and my family,
I was no more than a boy
In the company of strangers
In the quiet of the railway station,
Running scared, laying low,
Seeking out the poorer quarters
Where the ragged people go,
Looking for the places
Only they would know.

Asking only workman's wages
I come looking for a job
But I get no offers
Just a come-on from the whores
On Seventh Avenue.
I do declare
There were times
When I was so lonesome
I took some comfort there . . .

In the clearing stands a boxer
And a fighter by his trade.
And he carries a reminder
Of every glove
That laid him down
Or cut him till he cried out
In his anger and his shame:
'I am leaving, I am leaving.'
But the fighter still remains.

Paul Simon, 'The Boxer'

CHAPTER I

*Being the story of Adam's mother, the story of
Adam's father, of Adam's sister and of other
relatives*

And God remembered Rachel, and God hearkened unto her, and
opened her womb. And she conceived, and bare a son; and said,
God hath taken away my reproach: And she called his name Joseph
. . . And it came to pass, when Rachel had borne Joseph, that Jacob
said unto Laban, Send me away, that I may go unto mine own place,
and to my country. Give me my wives and my children, for whom I
have served thee . . . For it was little which thou hadst before I
came, and it is now increased unto a multitude; . . . and now when
shall I provide for mine own house also?

Genesis 30:22–30

I

If, in the middle of her year, late on a winter's night when the rain
first stormed, then drizzled, she stood outside herself and looked at
her dream, she had reason to be proud. What she had was good and
what she had she had shaped with her own hands, alone and
unaided. But she also had reason to be sad because alone and
unaided was what she was and how she often felt. Her son was gone,
her husband had left her and taken the good memories with him,
and her daughter was lost in the small traumas and complexities that
a young woman faces. Her family was no more; perhaps it never
really had been at all.

She had friends – good friends and some true as few friends are –
but they were, in a sense, in another of her worlds; they could not
enter this sadness or comfort her in it. Yes, a person is truly alone
when she dreams.

Adam's mother was born on the first day of spring in nineteen
thirty-five. She was the second and last child of a small businessman

and his wife. They lived in Red Butte, Nebraska. On the one side her grandfather was a Norwegian immigrant and a successful farmer; on the other, her grandfather was half French, half Dutch and the owner of a defunct goldmine in the Black Hills of South Dakota. He had won and lost a fortune a time or two and finally died leaving the small business which his son managed.

When Adam's mother was ten years old her father moved the family to California, first working for the government in the San Joaquin Valley and later buying a small roadside restaurant on highway 101 near Pacific Grove.

She began her college studies at the University of California at Berkeley and had completed the first two years before she met and married Adam's father. He was her complete antithesis but she married him, as young girls will, because he was exciting and strange. He smelled right. She left her studies uncompleted and began a new life as a military man's wife. She felt her disappointment early but in her perseverance quickly covered it over. She soon bore two children and they were her life and joy and pride for many years to come. Adam was the first child; and a daughter, Barbara, was fifteen months younger.

Adam's mother was an intelligent woman and she knew that her children would one day grow up and no longer need her constant care and concern; so when her daughter's babyhood was past she took a job. They were living in England then and her job as a typist in a secretarial pool helped to alleviate her loneliness and doubt. She was an outgoing woman by nature and it was not until after she took her job that she fully realized just how lonely, except for her children, she had become. Adam's father was an untalkative man and often sullen in disposition. The companionship of other women, American and English, was therapeutic. The typing was monotonous but this too was good because, for an intelligent and ambitious person, monotony grows slowly or quickly into dissatisfaction which in turn causes her ambition to thrive and grow. And so it happened with Adam's mother.

Now Americans, because they are a democratic people and because the land they inhabit has always been longer and wider than they were, are a people in constant flux. No generation should be measured solely by the one preceding or succeeding it because each is a different people. During these years the principle of flux was nowhere more dramatic in its staging or powerful in its implications than in the women's movement that was destined to expose the very roots of American society. A new wave had been born and had grown with the women of the two preceding generations, now it was to crest; and in time it was destined to throw this generation's own daughters struggling like wash upon an unknown shore. But now, these were the years of cresting and Adam's mother was not one to be far from the center of her generation's greatest drama. Dissatisfaction and ambition may have been the point from which she started, but it was not long before her driving force was a strange kind of patriotism, a patriotism that could only arise in America during this generation.

When she and her budding family again moved back to the States it was this time to Montana – Great Falls, Montana. There was a university there and it did not take her long to decide that she wanted that Bachelor of Science in Business which she had given up six years earlier. And in three years, between children and classes, and with what seemed like little support from either heaven or home, she had it. But now it wasn't sufficient; the patriotism had become a fever and the dream had taken on a life of its own. With this, however, her marriage had also begun to show the strain of stretching beyond its capacity. By mutual agreement Adam's father took the opportunity of a year's service in Turkey and Adam's mother, with the children, went back to Nebraska and at Lincoln took a Master's in Business Administration with an eye to teaching.

The campus life had grown on her; in it there was both an excitement and a security that marriage had only promised. Although it was hard to supply the needs of two children and to squeeze an eighteen-month program into less than a year, it was the dream's first real test and proof; determination and fervor succeeded where anything less would have failed.

When Adam's father returned from Turkey he attended her graduation ceremony and afterward the whole family moved to Massachusetts where he would be stationed and where she had been offered her first teaching job. But although the family was together again, it was not whole; never truly substance, it was now only a reflection. It was something for those who don't look too closely; and something for the children whom we would not have know, but who always know even when they don't know they know. Adam's mother's life centered around the private New England college where she taught, and the children were brought into that orbit.

Adam's father again took an opportunity of a six-month tour of duty in Europe and not long after volunteered for service in Viet Nam. Adam's mother took the children back to Nebraska and began to work on her Doctorate. She was hardened now: a change and a challenge, alone, would never again be a threat.

She was made the Head Resident of a women's dormitory and the children had a home. Their neighborhood was a university campus and their neighbors university students; they grew a little faster for it. She created a rhythm for them which included their father away in a war – but that was exciting and they were still a family.

In the children's eyes her classes and the war seemed to conclude together and the family was reunited for a short time. But Adam's mother had her dissertation to research and write and so had to travel for a year. As a result Barbara was sent to live with her mother's parents while Adam and his father traveled across the country together to an Air Base near Seattle.

Adam's mother traveled constantly, her work was interviews and writing; but, although the dream was real, it was lonely without the children. Loneliness is a part of dreams made real but only for a time. She visited the children when she could and talked about being together. That year was difficult but, like all the others before it, it was soon past. She had her degree, and a career, and her children were growing up and they were all together again. But the promised time together was not easy. The children had not lived as a family for a long time and they did not really know what it was like – it was strange. They were both entering adolescence and that was strange too. For Adam's mother it was all she could do to try to keep together a family that was prone to flying apart. Nor was she successful, for the next year her job was in Ohio and her husband's was in New York. Barbara lived with her, but Adam went with his father because he was quarrelsome and often angry and he needed a father even at the expense of not having a mother. It saddened Adam's mother but it had to be done. So many things had to be done.

A woman cannot say that she loves one of her children above the other – not in complete honesty – for both are her children. But a mother makes her mistakes with her first child; he is her learning and her growing and it is not possible to let go her mistakes, her youth and growing without tears and secret weeping. Adam was on the threshold of growing up. He had begun to make decisions for himself and was stubborn in them, even, perhaps especially, against a mother's entreaty and a mother's anger. This was the beginning of a long parting; only if she was strong would there be a returning.

She turned her anger and her tears inward and brought them forth again in a zeal in her classes. She was like a woman in love, enraptured; and she was good. The students felt her love and they accepted it, and perhaps they still feel it from time to time today. They felt as though a comet had been among them; perhaps one had. The light and the heat were in evidence and so was the movement, for after two short years she accepted the rank of Assistant Professor at Humboldt State in Eureka, California. Her star had risen.

Adam's father retired from the military that same year and he and Adam also came to Eureka. In an odd sort of way he was eclipsed as the head of the household. But a man like Adam's father must be the head of the house and his silent authority must reign. If it didn't there would be anger – an anger long held in the depths of his soul, an anger that could rend asunder. His silence did not reign in this new house; ambition did, and ambition was a thing Adam's father had very short store of. It was something he didn't understand, and what he didn't understand he left.

While Adam's mother lived her dream in the lecture halls and the office open to students more hours than most, Adam's father had to redesign his. He did the only reasonable thing he could though it nearly crushed Adam's mother and almost sent the star spinning earthward; in the end it brought the full weight of her hatred down upon him. He chose another woman and sued for divorce. She did not, could not have expected this. It confused her and hurt her in a way that nothing even the least bit expected could have. They had talked about a divorce years before when they both realized that the marriage was not giving either of them what they wanted or needed, but they had decided against it, perhaps because of the children and perhaps for other reasons. Her marriage was unsuccessful – she knew that and accepted it and thought that he did also – but she had grown used to it. In her shock and her reeling she almost joined a convent.

But she never would have made a successful nun. She was indeed religious and reverent, but there was just too much passion and love for the world in her soul, she needed to be engaged in constant activity – visibly fruitful activity – and, too, the patriotic fervor with which she committed herself to her projects and her dreams often humbled the reverent woman's humility. No, she would not have made a successful nun. But it wasn't this knowledge that stopped her reeling thoughts of such things; it was Adam's father's audacity. He was a bold man, there was no doubt, but he rubbed salt into her open wounds when in court he asked that she settle on him. When he won – the court ordered a forty-thousand dollar settlement – her anger raged and the bitterness seeped from her pores. It crept into her speech no matter how much she might try to hold it back. He had more than insulted her, he had insulted the very progress of America and her patriotism could not have conceived of a more vile treachery. That patriotism roared and its rage sought a path just as mountain torrents seek dry *arroyos*.

If she had been careful and uncommitted in her campus politics thus far, she was anything but that now. Campus politics is a dangerous game, especially for an untenured Assistant Professor – a middling rank on the official totem pole. If a person begins to play this brand of poker she has to ante up her job security and raise with her official reputation (and there are few groups more prim and proper, more stratified, than the small bands of Doctors at State Universities). But her pain was deep – her pruning had almost been a killing – she was ready to bloom. And bloom she did. In a year she was tenured and in three she was elected Faculty President and raised to a full Professor to boot. The dream had at last reached its fulfillment.

Pride and sadness: such is the wool that dreams are woven of.

And had she gone to the window she would have noticed that the rain had stopped, the clouds had drifted away, and the stars had appeared in the sky again. But she didn't do this, she didn't notice, for she had begun to dream a new dream.

2

Adam's father was indulgent with himself but not very much so with others. He was the kind of man who wanted to feel the way he wanted to feel when he wanted to feel that way; and if anyone came in his way he would snarl like a dog who you knew would bite even though you knew it never had yet. Every time he didn't bite, you knew that it was due to your own wise handling of the situation – everyone, when they left Adam's father, left him with that almost-full feeling of having faced a challenge, overcome it and learned something in the process. It was not a bad feeling at all.

Sometimes Adam's father liked to feel a peon upon whom the system and the system's managers were trampling with every step. He would read in the morning paper what they had done to him yesterday, and in the evening paper what they had done to him today; and curse under his breath if no one was around, or out loud if anyone was. Sometimes, if he was in his peculiar kind of communicative mood he would say just exactly what the system's managers should have done. Sometimes what he said made sense – good home-grown common sense – and sometimes it didn't make any more sense than what the managers had done (but let no one give himself airs and say so).

Sometimes Adam's father liked to feel the master of his world and to condescendingly show its beauty and dimensions beneath the sweep of his hand to the apprentice at his side. At these times he had snowshoes on, or was kneeling in the stern of a two-man canoe, or perhaps was in the bed of his pickup preparing sleeping bags for the night. He didn't really mind teaching a person the things that he knew but he showed very little tolerance if they weren't learned the first time.

Usually, however, Adam's father liked to feel alone. He was a lonely man who cultivated a silence about him and the silence assured his being left alone. Occasionally the woman he married would, with apparent carelessness, cross the fields of his silence and cause him to redirect his attention. But women are fearless creatures and he indulged them for that very fearlessness; no child, and seldom another man, would be so foolish. He never allowed himself more than one or two friends at a time, and sometimes not even that.

But he did have two life-long friends who lived in the Frazier Valley of British Columbia. They had grown up together when their fathers all worked at a milk plant in Abbotsford; but now they were as different from each other as the seasons. No one of them could have endured another or another's life for more than a week, but each enjoyed the other's stories when they got together once every year or two and drank themselves into each other's lives – or at least to the extent that their own wives and families would allow them. Adam's father didn't usually drink – perhaps a glass of wine before dinner or a beer after work, never more – but he could be trusted to set himself a limit, exceed it and then forget that he had ever set one at all, when he was among these friends.

These wives knew how very thin the threads were that held this friendship together. They said so too. If the friends knew this they never showed it and if they heard their women they never listened. Each of these women knew (or imagined) how, deep within the recesses of her husband's soul, it must become more and more difficult, even frightening, with each passing year to hold to a friendship so tenuous, a friendship that must certainly one day dissolve; so they were never to be found too far from where the men met. The next room, they knew, was best, and on occasion they even managed to secure it; to this day they still try. While their mutual understanding of the situation has made them steadfast friends.

These three men had grown up together – every adventure during their first sixteen years was shared: fishing for tadpoles with molotov cocktails, the squashed rebellions from their fathers' rule, their first guns, the stories of their first girls: all those things that make for life-long friendship. But by sixteen, childhood was past and the tides of family history called each to his own. No man can escape – or even really wants to – the callings of his heritage, even though superficially he might seem to be doing exactly that.

Families are the clay that nations are made of and Adam's father and his childhood friends were the clay that families are made of. As each was called to account he began to play his part in his family's history, his part in a nation's history. The youngest among them began work full-time in the garage that his father had bought; eventually he married, inherited the garage and settled for good in their home town. The second, whose father managed the milk plant and whose grandfather had built it as he had built and sold a half-dozen others in the thirty years it took him to reach British Columbia from the Pasteur Institute in Bern, Switzerland, began work as a lumberjack and a drywaller until he had his stake. He graduated then to gambling in earnest. He bought or built one establishment after another – a bar and hotel on Victoria Island, a machine tool business in Edmonton, a tool rental business in Quesnel – and he was always on the verge of winning or losing half a fortune.

At sixteen, Adam's father joined the Canadian Air Force and spent the last two years of World War II at a supply depot in

Ottawa. After his four years in the Canadian service he went to the States, joined a marine unit in Washington, availed himself of service benefits and went to college in San Francisco for a year, dropped out, joined the US Air Force as a Buck Sergeant (because of his previous experience), married Adam's mother, and began a twenty-year career.

Adam's father's family history was one of men who had moved away and re-established themselves. There was nothing ambitious about them; they did what they did because situations forced them to. They were restless, and wherever they were there was something that they couldn't abide and so they didn't. The first Richards that anyone knew of had come from somewhere in Sussex, England, and it was said that he left both a mother and a wife behind when he found out he had married wrong. He walked out in the middle of an argument and boarded the ship. That was sometime in the early eighteenth century. A half-century later the Richards were established in two different Colonies and the Territory of Quebec. That was just before the Revolution broke out. By the time the British troops actually landed every Richards who really was one was in Quebec and heading west. The family lost a few, of course, but every family does; it's a family's curse to bear a son with ambition or a yen for fame. Such were cast out. It wasn't that the Richards hadn't any fight in them – indeed, every generation had more than most families – but they lacked a loyalty to great causes. They flowed with the tides of history, they didn't make them. They were interested in establishing a family on good land not too near a town, and not in establishing a country or even in changing the name of one. Let fools stand in ranks and fire volleys from muskets and rifles that sometimes fired and sometimes exploded. No Richards had yet died in that kind of battle. At one point, a few generations later, a rumor reached the Richards that a line from the son left back in the war had established a banking concern and was said to be worth ten millions. 'It wasn't the same family!' they declared, and laugh about it to this day.

For the past four generations the family had begun to move back and forth across the US–Canadian border; if a father was to be found on one side, his son was sure to be found on the other. They had left drafts and wars behind, had in one shady affair established a union, but for the most part had established farms and ferries. So it was no surprise when Adam's father went south, although his military connections were frequently questioned within the family.

Adam's father was no hero. It was true that he had served in three wars: the first one as a kid of sixteen and the last one as a volunteer, but he was no hero. Heroes were fools. He served in the supply lines like a trader bordering on Indian Territory, a frontiersman without the fuss. He had seen commands return from the field only two-thirds the size they went out and carrying their wounded back with them. It was fine to see these things, but a man had to be stupid or crazy to live them. And Adam's father was neither – the Richards were in his blood.

True, he had volunteered for service in Viet Nam but the war was on its last legs by then and it was one hell of a lot saner there than it was living with Adam's mother. The woman had what she needed and still wasn't satisfied. There were the two kids – and if she wanted a job, fine; let her take a job and bring a little more in. God knows it couldn't hurt. But this pushing, striving after dreams, was like purposely rocking a steady boat in calm water and that was damn stupid. He couldn't talk to her about it. He was too sure and she was a patriot. She was too proud and determined, like those kids – boys most of them – who went into the field in full regalia sure that somewhere in those trees was glory. But if they found it they never came back to talk about it. No, maybe a divorce was best after all.

The divorce finally happened because of a woman who, at least, wasn't crazy with ambition. She had a good job and two boys of her own. She was satisfied with a man, her sons, a house and her job. Adam's father could finally relax a bit. The divorce was only reasonable. He had tried and damn hard; twenty years he had tried to understand an almost patriotic madness. In the last years he had even gone to college and had got an Associate Degree, but it didn't work – he couldn't understand. There was something in the marrow of his bones – no, in his blood – that wouldn't let him understand. So if, after all that, a thing doesn't work, a man's got to stop and begin something that will work. And Adam's father did.

When the papers were finalized and the settlement arranged, he bought another house, remarried and settled down at last. He took a part-time job driving a school bus and he went to the public library three times a week. In the summers he drove the buses for the volunteer patrols called in to fight the forest fires. And he was satisfied.

'Adam! . . . Put your brain in gear before you engage your mouth! . . . Adam! . . . Adam!' the words rang through his head like bells on a clear night resounding again and again. Adam was thirteen years old and wandering through a field somewhere in Massachusetts: not too far from home, a field that was very quiet, with a railroad line running across it and stacks of old ties and great, round, rolling – tables, they looked like – but they must have been for wire or cable or something.

'Adam . . .', and the rebuke came again. He wanted to crawl into the maze of tables, stacked three high, and never come out. Then his mother had to say, 'Listen, honey, don't be so hard on him. He's only a boy . . . he's only a boy . . . only a boy . . .'

'Damn it, I am not ONLY A BOY; and you stay out of it!' he muttered under his breath. His father was silent then and his mother looked shocked. 'Why don't you both just go away and leave me alone.'

Yes, that's what he should have said and just walked off leaving them wondering if he was ever going to come back. But instead, what he did was try very hard not to cry (he didn't either) and at last said that he was going to a friend's house. Then he had come here; he had been here before and he knew that it was a good place to talk things out.

Adam knew that he had to decide whether he was angry or insulted or what. He had decided one thing already: that it was going to be a long time before he had anything important to say to either of them again. They would be very careful what they said to him once they realized that he could be silent too.

Adam's mother and father both loved him. But in different ways. Psychologists often tell us how a mother's love differs from a father's. They say that a mother's love is unconditional, all-embracing, completely unselfish and given even when it is shunned. They conjure up in our minds a picture of a woman who calms a crying infant by giving it her breast or who carries a child (and an unlovable creature to any observing stranger) unmeasured miles on her back or her hip. This is in direct contrast, they say, to a father's love. He loves from a distance, often not even realizing that he has begotten a son or a daughter until the kid has been talking and walking a blue streak for a full four years. Then something clicks, perhaps pride. His first words in reference to his heir are always, 'What, my son did that? Why, I'll be damned!' or 'Christ, that's my daughter who said that!' Then, they go on to tell us, his love awakens; but it is a love that demands performance. His affection, it seems, is strongly and naturally supported by the twin pillars of reward and punishment.

They are right, in the main. It is indeed a wonder to sit in any public place and watch the families pass. Man is a unique creature because he naturally – to all observing, unthinkingly – gives a full generation to raise the next generation. Both the mother and the father participate fully in this illogical scheme. Two people who have come together, seldom with the thought of a child foremost in their minds, and who, when suddenly presented with one, give their lives, their fortunes and their futures to that bawling, peeing mass of uncontrolled and essentially uncontrollable responses. They are both martyrs and deserve a martyr's reward though I occasionally wonder if they ever receive it.

A mother's love is like honeysuckle, as thick and rich as honey itself. It pours. Although we may with one eye see it as the ideal of unselfish love, we must, with the other eye, see it as selfishness itself. These two are not opposites at all; but each is carefully concealed deep within the other. A mother's unselfish love grips a child with soft and coaxing hands when he is most vulnerable and never releases him again. Has there ever lived a child who, being some distance from his mother's home, has not received a sticky-sweet letter from her in which she blatantly and uncompromisingly tells him that she is thinking of him on his birthday? These letters are always signed: YOUR MOTHER or some no less emphatic variation. The child, of course, had been much too busy to remember that last Tuesday was his birthday. He smiles and feels warm; and when he is older he will be able to understand and explain that he loves his mother for that thick, too-rich stickiness, even though he is searching for something else.

A father's love is cruel. It is the love of one spirit for another – the promise of the spirit's future. The spirit is always cruel. A father, for example, never sends his child a birthday letter – although we do, on occasion, see where a father has been compelled to sign his name at the bottom of a mother's letter. There is always a grease smudge beside his name and you know that his thoughts were really with the

'*A mother's love is like honeysuckle . . . a father's love is cruel*'

(A pair of alchemists, *Mutus liber* (1702); The Beinecke Rare Book and Manuscript Library, Yale University)

ball-bearing or the chain. This usually solicits some sharp comment from the mother who doesn't understand the spirit, and a closed-mouth grin from the child who does. A father never writes or sends these kind of letters because, frankly, he is hard-pressed to remember the year that his child was born, let alone the day. ('Let's see, it wasn't long after signing that first mortgage . . . no, I didn't have the pickup then . . . oh, hell, I don't remember.') If a father doesn't live in a society that constantly demands facts and dates and numbers to process his every action he doesn't even remember his own birthday. After all, the spirit is not really concerned with birthdays, is it? The spirit is only interested in teaching itself about itself: very unselfish, deep down and concealed. The spirit will burn you, teaching you about fire; or cut you, teaching you about knives or the thin edge of a blade of grass; it will clothe you, but not too warmly, to teach you about the north wind or the rain. The spirit will teach you secrets but it doesn't care about you at all; it's complete concern is to renew itself within you. The child accepts this but he is searching for something else.

Adam did crawl in between the ties and the tables that day; and he sat there until the sun set behind the trees. He was not able to decide, however, whether he was angry at his father and insulted by his mother, or if it was his spirit that was insulted, or if he was just plain angry at being stuck. From that day forward he carefully rehearsed his words inside his mind before he spoke.

4

Of the two children, Adam and Barbara, Barbara remembered things while Adam never forgot them. If, within the family, there was something of some importance that needed to be remembered or if a person wanted to be reminded of something, Barbara was the one they wanted. Everyone knew (even Adam) that Adam could be trusted to forget everything except what he deemed important. What Adam deemed important was a peculiar assortment of facts and ideas and emotions – an odd conglomeration of things that made no whole sense to anyone except Adam himself. He judged the significance of an occasion, as he understood it, either important or not, but couldn't care less about the occasion itself. It was soon discovered, for example, that unless it was essential that Adam be there, it was to no one's advantage to drag him along to weddings or other ceremonies. He could be trusted to stare stupefied when he wasn't supposed to, and not even be looking when he was supposed to.

That Adam never forgot was to prove his greatest blessing and his greatest curse: he needed none to remind him who he was – he never forgot. He was human.

When Adam was four years old and very busy with his work, Barbara was three years old and very busy with hers. But Barbara's work seemed so often to be to come up to Adam and interrupt him. 'Adam. Adam . . . Adam look what I found . . . Adam look.'

'Go away Barbie, I'm busy with this.'

'Adam. Adam look . . . Adam!' and she would begin to hit him. 'Adam pay attention to it!'

'Go away. Stop that.'

'Adam, look.'

Then Adam would hit her back and as she began crying he would say half-aloud and resentfully, 'I told you to leave me alone.'

This sequence was repeated many times and always seemed to continue thus: 'Mommie, Mommie,' Barbara would wail through her tears, 'Adam hit me.'

It always concluded badly. Now that Adam's mother was involved it took the shape of 'ADAM!' and ended in trouble. That is, it always concluded badly except for that last time it occurred. The sequence changed slightly that time and a different justice was dispensed. It went something like this:

'Mommie, Mommie, Adam hit me back.'

'Ah, huh. Why were you hitting him?'

Silence.

Now, it is hard to say what Adam learned from this, but he didn't forget it. Adam had still not forgotten it three years later when he convinced Barbara that a flea market was a place where they sold trained fleas. With hidden glee he described every detail of the fleas' performances he had seen. Adam had still not forgotten some six years later when Barbara and he divided their 7-UP (they were allowed one can between them per day). One of them would divide it very carefully and the other had choice of the glasses. Adam would pour his back into the can and challenge Barbara to see who could drink all of his portion first. She would accept and the race was on. She always won. Although Adam always lost he seemed to have a full half-can of 7-UP in his hand for the next half-hour. When

Barbara finally realized that she would always win, the races were over. Adam finally felt revenged, his vendetta ended.

5

Through the years of his childhood Adam could be very angry but probably not to an extent completely uncommon in American boys. His anger would pass quickly and he never knew hatred. But once. And that once was enough. He hated with a hatred so deep that it poisoned his soul for a time.

His grandmother and he did not get along from the first. Perhaps it was that her world was crude and his refined; whatever the reason, there was a natural animosity between them. Adam and Barbara were staying with their grandparents during a school holiday; Adam was perhaps eight at the time. The scene was the dinner table and revolved around a dish of asparagus which Adam refused to eat even when ordered to. He knew what it tasted like and he knew that he did not like it. Then his grandmother said that he was 'making faces' at the asparagus. His face would never hide his thoughts. Later this would prove an asset in developing a habit of honesty but on this night it proved his undoing.

His punishment for not having a poker-face was to be whipped with his grandfather's belt. His grandmother ordered it so. And so it was. Adam had never been struck before or since; even Adam's father who, with his evil eye, could turn a person stone-cold with the fear of violence unleashed (indeed, Adam needed to read the story of Medusa but once to understand the fear she inspired), even Adam's father had never struck him.

Adam hated his grandmother for this. His hatred was deep and strong and he never again spent another night under her roof. This was an added burden for Adam's mother but, although she could not condone such an intense contempt between her mother and her son, she respected it and did her best to keep the two well apart.

Adam was satisfied with his hatred. It never outwardly affected his other relationships or any part of his life other than that which it controlled so completely. Except, perhaps, that it contributed to his general wariness of people. It wasn't until some ten years later that Adam's hatred subsided. Even then, he could never bring himself to like the woman.

Adam had other relatives too. But they played little part in his life.

18

He was not cold, but distant, with relatives. There was the grandfather who had used his belt on Adam and whom Adam's mother loved – almost revered – so deeply. This grandfather died of lung cancer one Christmas Day. After the funeral, Adam's mother declared her father a saint – she apparently felt no need to wait for the official canonization – but Adam knew that he was not a saint because no saint could have been convinced by a woman to strike a child as this man had.

Adam had another grandfather whom he liked much more. Perhaps it was that Adam only knew him after his wife had died and when he lived alone on the second floor and attic of his house near the railroad yard. Or perhaps it was because his grandfather was nearly deaf and used a hearing aid which worked well when it was turned on. Adam had often seen this old man, when tired of the talk and society which he was compelled to attend, secretly reach into his shirt pocket where the control to his hearing aid was kept and turn the instrument off. Adam loved the old man for that, and vowed that one day he would have a hearing aid which he could turn off also. Perhaps, too, it was that his grandfather had been hunting once when he was young and that his shotgun had exploded unexpectedly and had all but torn off his right arm just above the elbow. Adam's grandfather had tied his own tourniquet with his teeth and stumbled out of the woods. He reached a river and hailed two men in a passing boat before he collapsed. They quickly got him into their boat and headed down river to intercept the steamer that plied those waters. When they met the steamer the doctor on board took over and amputated the arm. Adam thought that this was a wonderful story; even at a young age Adam was an incurable romantic. He loved to watch his grandfather tie his shoelaces (the old man would never wear slip-ons, nor would he tolerate any help with these kinds of things) or cut the meat on his dinner plate or play cribbage. Adam's grandfather taught him how to cheat at cribbage and how to turn a baked potato into a smashed potato right on his plate with only salt and pepper and a little milk. Adam and his grandfather liked each other very much.

One day, some years later, when Adam was not really attending high school any longer, he heard from Barbara that their grandfather was dying and that their parents had left for his home in British Columbia two days before. Adam immediately began hitch-hiking north from Eureka. But he didn't get very far along the interstate before the rain clouds which had looked threateningly over the earth for the past three days began to hurl a cold, whipping rain from the skies. Adam stood by the side of that highway in the rain and the cold until the sun set. He was destined not to be with his grandfather this time. Then, like a mongrel soaked to the skin and with his tail between his legs, he returned to his loft in a house near the railroad yard. He had caught a bad cold and spent the next three days in bed with only the hallucinations of *Crime and Punishment* to comfort him.

When his parents returned from Canada Adam was asked to choose his inheritance from among his grandfather's effects. He chose a watch and a photograph of his grandfather as a two-year-old child. In the photograph his grandfather was wearing a little girl's dress so that the fairies wouldn't think him a boy and steal him away.

CHAPTER II

*Being of Adam's childhood travels and their effect
upon him*

And Jacob dwelt in the land wherein his father was a stranger, in the
land of Canaan . . . Joseph, being seventeen years old, was feeding
the flock with his brethren; and the lad was with the sons of Bilhah,
and with the sons of Zilpah, his father's wives: and Joseph brought
unto his father their evil report. Now Israel loved Joseph more than
all his children, because he was the son of his old age: and he made
him a coat of many colours. And when his brethren saw that their
father loved him more than all his brethren, they hated him, and
could not speak peaceably unto him.

Genesis 37:1–4

I

Had Adam been born the child of an aristocratic or caste society
where all social relationships and activities are tightly structured,
perhaps then he would have known a stronger and more classical
feeling of kinship. But Adam was the child of a democratic nation
where social bonds are loose and constantly readjusted as society
fluctuates. Nor was Adam born the child of a democracy in its
prime, but of one in its decay: a time when loose social bonds are
often cast off completely. Nearly a century before Adam's birth a
great American president had warned his people that a house
divided against itself cannot stand, but little did he suspect then that
one day every house in the nation he loved would be divided against
itself, or that each within every house would try to stand alone.
Strong families make strong nations, but by the last half of the
twentieth century America had few strong families, few great
families on which she might depend for strength as a tree depends
upon its roots. America's roots had been poisoned by the very thing
she had become, and they decayed. Adam, and many American

children, grew to maturity during these years with next to no sense of family at all.

Although he would not for many years recognize the gap in his life that a family should rightly fill, he would always know of homelessness. Slowly, as years passed and experiences broadened, he grew to accept and love the freedom and independence of wandering. Adam wandered, even as gypsies might wander, through settled people's lives and into and out of gypsy encampments; there was nothing to hold him to any one place or people. Adam was born a gypsy among gypsies at one such encampment. Its name was Travis Air Base and it was near Sacramento on the river where gold was first found. He was born in an auspicious place. Not long after his birth his mother was back on her feet and the family was moving. They wandered to a distant country called Sussex, from where his people had first come many, many years before. He also saw where his mother had come from: a small town in the middle of America in wheat fields wider than a hundred other places put together. When the family paused there she had a daughter and so now Adam had a sister who came from the wheat fields also.

Adam met many people in the country called Sussex: some were other gypsies from America, some were gypsies from Sussex, and some were just plain people who lived in Sussex. The people who lived in Sussex spoke a different language: it was like his own language, but not quite, and so it was different, even though they called it English too. Soon Adam learned the language so well that the people who lived in Sussex sometimes said that he spoke it better than they themselves did. Adam liked that, and he liked them; but Adam's family were gypsies and they had to move again.

This time the family moved to Montana, a place in America that Adam's mother said was close to the place where she had come from. But it wasn't where she had come from because there were lots of mountain ranges and cattle herds in Montana, but there wasn't any wheat. Here Adam had to go to school for the first time because the law said so, but, more important, because his mother said so. He went to a Catholic school where the teachers were called nuns and slapped children on their hands with rulers if they didn't stand like statues when somebody blew a whistle that a person couldn't hear if he were playing; and they made people sit in wastepaper cans if you asked a question and they said something and then you said they didn't answer your question. Adam didn't like that and Adam's father didn't like that either. So they moved again.

But Adam's father moved to a country called Turkey which was probably near Sussex because it too was across the ocean; while Adam and his mother and his sister went to Nebraska where his mother came from and they lived at a university. At the university everybody had to go to school, even people as old as Adam's mother. Adam's mother said that she liked school but he thought that she was crazy because he knew that he hated it. That was all that Adam did at the university: hate school and eat breakfast and dinner in a big university cafeteria. Adam was very happy when his mother fell into a fountain on graduation day and his father came back from Turkey and took them all to another state called Massachusetts.

In Massachusetts Adam's gypsy family lived in a house on a hill that was owned by an old Greek fisherman and the road to their house was called Maynard Road after the ship's Captain who captured Blackbeard the Pirate. On the next street there lived a Portuguese family with a daughter named Maria with whom Adam fell in love. But that didn't work out well because they were too young. While they lived in the house on the top of their own little hill Adam's father went to wander in Europe. Adam would have liked to go along also but when he asked if they all might go, his father replied that the schools in Europe weren't very good. Always the schools! How Adam hated schools. He knew that this was only an excuse because almost everything that he learned, he learned outside of school; and he often said so. One day he would go to Europe himself and he might even leave school to do it.

When Adam's father returned from Europe the family moved to the Air Base where his father worked, but Adam didn't like the place much. The Air Bases had begun to look more and more like bases of box-buildings and less and less like gypsy encampments. Adam's father didn't like it there either so he went to war in Viet Nam and the family went back to the university in Lincoln, Nebraska.

This time they lived in a women's dormitory where Adam's mother was the Head Resident. But Adam was the only man in the building and he 'didn't get no respect'. Sometimes he would go up the stairs to one of the upper floors and on each level he would call out 'Man on Floor' as was the convention so that the women might know what state of undress they could wander around in. It was inevitable that before Adam had fulfilled his charge and had returned to the ground floor, some head, securely wrapped in a towel – these ladies more often looked like Sikh warriors about to drive you from out Mother India than American co-eds engaged in their studies, so often were they washing their hair – would sound the attack with 'Boy on Floor'. Then a fit of giggling would erupt from any number of the closed or half-closed doors. Adam knew his rights and one of them was that he was not to be laughed at; but he was no fool either, and so was not going to face an entire floor of Amazons, who looked like they were painted for war, alone. So he would bravely assert again, 'Man on Floor!' and wisely run down the stairs to the security of the public domain. Once safe again, he would soothe his bruised ego by recalling Dr Fate's immortal wisdom: he who fights and runs away lives to fight another day.

Soon, however, Adam's father returned from the war in Viet Nam and told stories of bombing raids and strange customs; he only told them once, when Adam would have had them told over and over again. All that Adam's father said was that Adam had been with women too long and that the two of them needed to spend the year together in Washington. Adam needed no convincing.

They bought a Toyota Landcruiser in Minneapolis and traveled across the country together. The trip was a difficult one for Adam because he had to learn his father's harsh ways anew. He had forgotten that cuttingly critical voice that bit into his memory and stayed there like a bulldog in a fight. He had become soft with the pampering of so many women. The questions he asked were the questions a girl might ask. He asked if the bumps on his breast meant he had breast cancer. His father's uncompromising opinions soon set him right and taught him how to effectively badger himself over his own stupidities.

On this trip Adam also became painfully aware that he didn't see things. Later he would console himself with the knowledge that although he often missed the details he had developed a masterful vision of the greater design. But then it was only that he didn't see things. How often would an eagle or a hawk circle overhead, a jackrabbit, a fox, or a mule deer race for a bush and his father say, 'Look there!' pointing past Adam's nose. He would look as quickly as he could, and everywhere he could, but there was nothing. His eyes could not readjust to focus on the minute so quickly.

The first times this happened he would say, 'I didn't see it. What was it?' but he soon learned to say nothing at all because his father always cut deeply with:

'Jesus Christ Almighty, boy! Were you asleep? You don't seem to see a damn thing.'

By the time they arrived in Seattle they had grown used to one another again and Adam was learning to be like his father in many ways. But there were some things in which Adam refused to be like him. That year passed quickly. It was one of coin collections and country music radio, Perry Mason on the television, TV dinners and pot-pies, frozen filet-mignon wrapped in a slice of bacon and a cinema once a week. Adam and his father developed a very regular life and they needed no other people – books and the radio satisfied them.

However, Adam's mother and sister were coming for Christmas and they expected a house to be ready for them. Adam's father, and therefore Adam too, had been a little lax in that department because they had encamped at a roadside motel and were just as much at home there as they needed to be. Adam was a confirmed traveler now. He was confident that he could go anywhere, live anywhere, and among any people, without any problems. Traveling was in his blood and he knew that when the day came that his father finally settled down (and that day must eventually come) he would keep traveling. Somehow the roads wouldn't be the same, their purpose not fully fulfilled, if there wasn't a Richards on them. By now Adam had developed a habit which he has to this day. No sooner does he come to a new place and settle the question of where he is going to sleep than he steps out into the sunset and gazes at the horizon, deep in tomorrow's journey.

Adam felt his homelessness as a child but hid it in its own romance until it seldom sprang up at all. There was something nostalgic and warming about a home – like freshly-baked bread – but there was more to be pitied about those who enjoyed its privileges as granted rights and grew fat in their satisfaction and comfort. They knew nothing of the wandering life.

For Adam even the traditional family holidays had lost most of their savor. Adam's father finally decided on a house for Christmas, but that's all it really was: just a house for Christmas. The women were comforted by the house, for what that was worth. Adam was ready to move again. There was somehow gain by moving and only loss by being settled. And, to Adam's delight, they did move again.

Adam and his father to up-state New York and his mother and sister to Ohio.

2

Not long after Adam and his father settled in New York something occurred that nearly frustrated the entire move for him but which made clear an idea that he had only played with until then. The move had gone well – it was the best possible kind of move: from one end of the country to the other – they had a house on an Air Base outside the city of Rome and Adam had taken up his studies at a new school. Then, one day, when he was walking the corridors of the school from one class to another he suddenly came face-to-face with a girl he had known in Seattle. Her name was Alisha Barnnet and the two of them had been friends and rivals in their math classes and the district-wide competitions. They always got along well and Adam liked her as much as could be expected. She was an intelligent, rather plain-looking girl, tall and thin; she enjoyed her studies, and would always be intelligent.

There are many ways in which people are categorized and classified and Alisha would always fit into this one way. She would be called 'intelligent'. Although this particular way was as good as any other and certainly better than some, still it was only one way; Adam was not going to allow himself to be classified in any one way alone.

Alisha, as was both normal and proper, was happy that here, in these strange surroundings, was someone she knew. She immediately began to chat. Adam was polite but cold. Inside he was aghast that fortune could deal him such a hand. When they turned away from each other Adam was vehemently muttering vile curses against her, against a God he was not sure he believed in, and against destiny which he was sure he believed in. When he moved, you see, he took full advantage of it. Never content with himself, he used these opportunities to become a new individual. He would develop a new manner of speech, affect a new style of dress and deportment, find a different kind of friend, and actively seek fresh experiences which before he had only been allowed to imagine because of the tight little boxes that people tried to enclose him in.

He had to decide exactly what he was going to do; Lady Luck had thrown him a heart when his suit was spades and he had to decide

26

how to play it. Here was someone who knew him, or at least knew who he had been, and who would, if she were let, still try to think of him in that way. He knew that would be dangerous; on top of everything else, Alisha was a minister's daughter which (he intuitively knew) completely crippled her chance of understanding what was going on. He simply could not afford to have anyone thinking of him as an intelligent and scholarly student because that was not how he was planning to direct this scene of his life. It was HIS life.

In everything except math, which he still had cause to enjoy, Adam had enrolled in middle-level courses which he knew would do little to distract him from his chief study: that group of students who were given prestige and place by all the others because they were 'cool'. Confidence was what Adam was studying. Already he had maneuvered a change in his classes that caused a complete rearrangement of his schedule. He would have to check out of each class that he was now in and check into others; he was going to make full use of this bit of wizardry once he was officially out of the classes, and delay his re-entry for a month or so. He would join the blackjack and poker games that were held beyond the football fields.

No; it couldn't be helped, there were too many plans and opportunities. Although Alisha was a nice girl, Adam could not give her the chance to keep him from changing, from learning, because of her preconceptions. Adam decided what he had to and stiffened himself against the hurt that Alisha felt when he avoided and shunned her. But she was 'intelligent' and soon learned that he had changed. She decided that she didn't really know him at all; and she was right.

This incident served to convince Adam of a thing which he had come to suspect. Becoming a person was constant change and struggle, a willingness to throw away all that he had learned and believed, both of himself and of the world, when that became a necessity. Though this was mercenary when it hurt others, Adam knew that there was a spirit within him that was struggling to emerge from the shades and shadows of society. He knew that he might have to try on many a cloak before he found one that fit, that he might have to seek out many different kinds of company before he found those who were family. Home was no longer a house with shutters and elm trees; home was an unexplainable concept of being who he really was, everywhere he was.

Adam yearned to move, yearned to change, yearned to become;

to be that one step closer. Adam yearned to finish becoming and be. Not infrequently, during those hours that Adam set aside for watching people – a time of expecting nothing and learning everything – an old man, with a grizzled, unshaven face and a shock of white hair, or with no hair at all but with a fluffy white beard, would wander by and Adam would study him carefully, watching every movement or inclination, every expression or shadow of a thought: he would watch to see if in his years this old man had attained wisdom. If he had, there would be no mistaking or denying it; if he had, Adam would seek and find a thousand meanings in his simplest acts. He became a student of the spirit, who gazed lovingly on his master. Adam's humility and love were accepted and he grew.

He grew fearless too. Challenging all that he knew, he had nowhere to stand – if a person sets himself apart from the earth, where can he set his feet? – but to do this, and still maintain intellectual honesty, he needed to believe in his own safety. A person need not necessarily attribute a cause to it, but he must be assured of it. This takes a strong ego and it builds fearlessness and confidence. If Adam did, at this point, attempt to name the cause of his assurance he allowed it to remain vague. In his own heart he called it destiny. The assurance Adam grew and the fearlessness he cultivated also allowed him to look beyond the end of things peacefully. Adam, in his yearning to grow and advance, could long to be an eighty-year-old man endowed with wisdom, and he could long for death – what was death, after all, but one stop closer to his goal of knowing himself – to face the unknown and grow in it.

3

It might be said that the world offers its children their choice of two kinds of an education: either a banker's education or a hero's education. Most children, either by choice or by forfeiting their choice, receive a banker's education and this is because the world must spin regularly on its axis. Bankers keep the world regular. Heroes, on the other hand, keep the world spinning. The world does not need so many hands to perform this second duty so if a child aspires to fill this position and to receive this education he must have an intense will and show extreme exertion. It is as if the world challenges him to break the bonds of a banker's education to prove his worthiness for the other.

Adam was one of those who broke the bonds. As he traveled the length and breadth of America he looked deeply at her and realized that he could receive an education as long and as wide as America herself. But if this was going to be, and Adam earnestly wanted it so, then he would have to take responsibility for it himself. He would have to learn from the inside and bravely defend his thoughts from the daily onslaught of other people's thought (which they would have him accept without a full examination). The only other choice was to surrender his thoughts and himself to the schools. But this was repugnance itself – he discovered early that he hated every minute behind a desk in a square room with twenty-five other children behind desks listening to a teacher who, as often as not, had not thought and did not care about whatever it was that she was trying to convince Adam and the other twenty-five children of – had Adam chosen this his own nature would have abandoned him, perhaps even hated him, and by its conspicuous absence would never have left him an hour's peace. Adam was young when these things happened, but somehow his heart understood them even if his mind could not express it. So, with both repugnance and fear, he chose what was really no choice at all.

Adam learned many things through his education: things that a hero needs to survive and to fulfill his destiny. I will begin by telling of goodbyes and of one goodbye that he would never let himself forget.

Glen was Adam's friend in Seattle, perhaps his only friend in Seattle. Glen was shy, quiet, sensitive like Adam, but a little more conservative in his thinking about the world. Glen was a Texan when he had to say what he was and where he was from, but really he was a military child like Adam and used to the military's gypsy ways. Friendships among military children have their own special flavor because each knows that inevitably his friend will one day receive word from his father that they are moving again. This was accepted and friendships were formed on this basis.

The time came when Glen had to move and the day chosen by his father happened to be a school day. This was usually easier because classes keep friends from the difficulties of long goodbyes; bonds were always severed as quickly and cleanly as possible. But Adam, through an almost studied neglect, cut this goodbye cleaner than was necessary. He over-played the uncaring manner. Glen's father came to the school on the appointed afternoon to pick him up. But before they left, Glen had one last thing to do. He went to Adam's classroom and stopped in the doorway saying that he had to go and expecting Adam to walk with him to the car. Adam was in the middle of a chess match – his latest enthusiasm. He looked up from the board and said, 'Goodbye. I hope you have a good trip.' No love, no malice, no emotion at all. Then he looked down at the game position again. But he could not concentrate on it; he could only see, inside his own mind, Glen turning away from the door, hurt, walking to the parking lot and getting into the car. Then Adam heard the car drive away as his opponent said, 'It's your move.' Adam lost that game.

Though he learned things backwards, he learned them deeply. Nor did he forget what he learned: he kept Glen's goodbye alive and writhing in his memory until goodbyes became natural. Essentially Adam already had the right idea but it was his manner that needed work. He knew that a person cannot hold on to anything. To try to do so was not only fruitless but invited a kind of death, a death either in oneself or in that which was held. Friendship was no different from a flower: to pick it and to keep it was to kill it. It might survive for a day, but come nightfall it would be dead. This was true, Adam knew, but manner was the question. Glen's hurt was the result of a bad manner. He had to learn how to love the field's flower in passing. And learn he did, though slowly and often painfully. The day would come when he could depart from a friend saying with confidence that they would meet again. Adam has said this very thing to me and he believed it so strongly and his eyes smiled with such love and sincerity that my doubts melted before they reached my lips.

Many things such as this Adam needed to learn. He learned of giving and receiving, of keeping no treasures, and of offering gifts. He learned that it was true and good that we were interdependent, but that we must none-the-less cultivate self-reliance. He learned that a person must not be afraid of receiving, because if he sincerely wants to give then he must first receive. This in just proportion: the greater his giving will be, then the longer he must be dependent and open to receiving. This was no easy thing to resolve for an American adolescent aching to be independent of his parents and free of the bonds which he was afraid might cage his soul.

Adam learned to have little of his own and often spoke of himself as having no more than a bed-roll. In the years to come he never left one dwelling-place for another with more than twenty pounds of belongings. He learned, for instance, one night on a beach in Baha, Mexico, that to have too much money in his pocket only resulted in a bad night's sleep. Not a night full of worry because of a possible theft (for Adam had never been robbed and probably never would be – there was something of an aura of *sanctity-that-protected* round about him) but a night of discomfort because of the bulge in his pocket that prevented his sleeping: a kind of modern-day version of the Princess and the Pea folktale with today's natural addendum that 'the first shall be last and the last shall be first'.

But even before this understanding was conferred he would frequently, spontaneously and religiously search through his collection of things and take everything that he was not using at that time aside. He saved nothing for the winter: no book that had sat unread for a month was spared. Everything not in immediate use was somehow not his and he felt that to keep it from its proper possessor was wrong. Adam had for a long time made frequent trips to the Salvation Army outlets; he never hesitated to give or take as he needed. Both giving and taking were needs and he grew to understand and accept them.

A natural ebb and flow of need was one thing, but offering gifts was another thing entirely. To offer something that he treasured with his heart was indeed difficult. To want to offer these things was not the difficulty, to find someone who truly understood the value of the treasure was. So it was that he gave the Néz Pierce purse to a certain twelve-year-old girl one Christmas, a dearly-loved book to a friend who had already read it, and the small jade tree that he had watched through two spring seasons to an eighty-year-old lady gardener. Such people were few among the many and he had to keep a sharp eye out for them. They became more treasured than the gifts because they were rarer than the rarest of gifts.

Adam learned about being a loner and about being alone. He set himself outside the world and then spent many years adjusting to that position. He was lonely for a very long time. But loneliness was a small price to pay for the privilege of being able to view every man's world from a position outside it. Because he held to no one and no one held to him he did not judge any other as good or bad, but simply watched. Judgement, he knew, came of itself and could not be forced. He could wait, just as the person who wants to hear something new must listen to much he already knows and must patiently wait. When the time of aloneness was past he would be well able to make decisions both for himself and for others (which is the greater responsibility).

To say that Adam was learning in his travels is to say that he was learning all things. Sometimes he despaired of being so young and so far from wisdom; but sometimes he rejoiced at having his whole life to reach for it. Not only does every learning facilitate the growth of every other, but nothing is unconnected with the rest of the world. Adam loved, above all other things, to find those hidden connections. He rejoiced when he found a frequent and direct link between things usually thought of as opposed and opposite. There was nothing so succulent as paradox. Adam first discovered these mysterious and mystic links as a child of ten and played with them as a child should.

He would lie on his bed and think secretly (pretending even to himself that he was not) of something that he wanted to have happen. After secretly ascertaining what it was he wanted, he would throw his whole strength into its opposite. If, for example, it was a trip he wanted to take, he would not admit this to himself but instead would concentrate on staying exactly where he was forever. What a wonderful game this was, and almost always rewarded: the trip would come about.

Adam's game of opposites reached a summit seven years later when he was in his final year of high school in Eureka, California. He was sitting alone at a table in the school cafeteria. The lunch-hour crowd and bustle had slowly melted away and only a few small groups were still sitting and talking. Adam had not eaten; he had been in no mood to eat: he was indulging one of his periodic patterns of despondency. He had grown pessimistic through his childhood and was now sarcastic in his appraisal of things. He was feeling more down than was usual and perhaps even more down than he ever had before. After all, what hope was there? Then one of the people across the room shifted – no, jerked – in his chair and shook his head as if shaking off one of those tingling sensations that can creep up a person's spine. And with that, Adam suddenly laughed – a hard gasping laugh that began only at the base of the jaw and not in the belly, but which traveled in both directions at once reaching the heart at precisely the same instant it reached the lips. Adam's pessimism was gone; suddenly vanished, never to return again.

Adam had dived to his lowest depths and had come out on top. He took his pessimism fully on, around, and discovered it optimism. It was a beautiful journey, he thought, as he rose from the table, offered a smile to all, and walked from the room.

CHAPTER III

*Being how Adam relates to the author the story of
his mystic apprenticeship to Dick Van Dyke; also of
his ambition to become Pope and of his dream of
raking leaves*

And Joseph dreamed a dream, and he told it his brethren: and they
hated him yet the more. And he said unto them, Hear, I pray you,
this dream which I have dreamed: For, behold, we were binding
sheaves in the field, and, lo, my sheaf arose, and also stood upright;
and, behold, your sheaves stood round about, and made obeisance
to my sheaf. And his brethren said to him, Shalt thou indeed reign
over us? or shalt thou indeed have dominion over us? And they
hated him yet the more for his dream.

And he dreamed yet another dream, and told it his brethren, and
said, Behold, I have dreamed a dream more; and, behold, the sun
and the moon and the eleven stars made obeisance to me. And he
told it to his father, and to his brethren: and his father rebuked him,
and said unto him, What is this dream that thou has dreamed? Shall
I and thy mother and thy brethren indeed come to bow down
ourselves to thee to the earth? And his brethren envied him; but his
father observed the saying.

Genesis 37:5–11

I

It was a Sunday evening, perhaps a little before seven. Dinner was
cooking and Adam could smell the aroma of chicken as it floated in
clouds from the kitchen. He was eight years old and lying in front of
the fire at his grandmother's house. The snow was four feet deep
outside and the wind howled at the window panes from time to
time.

As Adam watched the flames jump and flicker and disappear
above the slowly crumbling logs he thought of that afternoon's

Mass. He had served as an altar-boy and had been dressed in a black smock and a white lace blouse; he had his trousers on underneath the smock and wearing both had made it difficult to walk. But he had done everything he was supposed to do and had completed the long pattern of giving and taking from the priest successfully. It was a difficult ritual to memorize because everything was said in Latin so there were no clues (except the ones he made up himself) to tell when to do what. Adam had to watch the priest very closely.

Although they were only visiting his grandmother's town, Adam's mother had suggested that he serve, and then arranged it with the parish priest. He had done well and she was pleased and proud of him tonight. She was sitting in an armchair against the side wall behind him and was watching him – not the fire – Adam knew. He could feel her pride.

Adam had watched the priest carefully. He was an old man but not fat like many old men. On him the ankle-length white gown and the green velvet robe, with a gold cross that blazed from shoulder to shoulder, from collar to floor, rode in swishing majesty; he glowed with that unaffected royalty of a servant of God. Some priests did not have this same shine about them; it was said that he had been born a farmer's son. The people of Red Bluff, especially the Catholics, revered him and spoke of him only with the highest respect. Father Patrick was like one of the wooden saints – like Joseph who stood as high as a man on the left hand of the altar: Joseph, who always carried his carpenter's hammer – except that Father Patrick was alive and was walking and shining right there in Red Bluff.

Adam knew that a parish priest was not really very high in the hierarchy of the Church. He held all the authority in a town or maybe even a couple of towns, but above him were bishops and archbishops and cardinals. Above everyone in the whole world was the Pope. He was a truly great man, perhaps the greatest man of all.

'One day', Adam said to his mother, 'I'm going to be Pope.' He had spoken to his mother alone and not too loudly. But his grandmother must have been closer than he had thought because she interrupted, 'Not just anybody can become the Pope!' She spoke in her gruff tone with an effort at finality. She liked to, and so often spoke that way, especially to Adam. But Adam wasn't going to let it be at that.

'Anybody can too become Pope because he is elected from

between the cardinals, by themselves. And besides, I am not just anybody! Mom has said that I can be whatever I want to be; haven't you, Mama?' he threw his argument at his grandmother and then turned to his mother for support.

'He's right, mother.' She interceded on his behalf, then turned, 'But Adam, being the Pope is a very high calling.'

Then his grandmother blurted out again, 'Have you ever heard of anyone except an Italian becoming Pope?'

'Yes!' Adam shot back because he had just won, 'I've read that Frenchmen and Spaniards and even Germans have been Pope.'

'Trisha, you pamper him too much.' She snorted and went back to the fried chicken. Adam didn't like her at all. He'd have been willing to bet that even the chicken would taste better if his mother were cooking it.

'So I can if I want to, and maybe I will', Adam said half-aloud. His mother was smiling at him again, he knew.

But Adam never would become Pope.

2

Every child finds some one unique teacher in his life, that one person who makes his heart fly. But a hero needs even more: a superstar, a master, a wizard. Adam told me about his wizard. He said, 'I first met him when I was seven. My mother took us kids to the movie *Mary Poppins*. So many other-worldly things happened in it: first Julie Andrews came floating in on a wind (I don't think Victorian ladies actually flew as such – it wouldn't have been proper, all that jumping and swinging your arms about – but I guess they could float if they wanted to), then tables and chairs danced, and then, best of all, Dick Van Dyke came jumping over the rooftops in his sooty black suit, top hat, and broom in hand: he was a chimney sweep. And he was singing. He is always singing: never anything fancy, just some tune that he makes up on the spur of the moment. He is always happy; at least he has always been happy when I've met him. Anyway, up he comes, jumping across the rooftops singing Chim-chim-cherie, chim-chim-cheroo . . . and that was that. He cast a spell on me.

'I know he can too – cast spells – if he wants to, because I've seen him do it to other people: spells to make people carry on with their normal business and not even notice that he and I are jumping around trying to pick up altitude; one time – I remember very clearly – he cast a spell on everybody in a university quad. He put them all into a flying mood and there they all were looking just as silly as could be, jumping and bumping into each other, and giggling, when they should have been busy going to classes. He and I were hovering at about twenty feet, doubled-over and clutching our sides for the pain of laughing so hard until they all started bumping into us too. That's when we decided to pick up speed by hopping along the rooftops nearby, and set out to find a less crowded part of the sky. As far as I know, all those people are still flying around there; at least I never saw him take the spell off. But I imagine that after a while most of them just got tired and went on to class or, maybe, home to think about what had happened. Perhaps one or two of them are still flying.

'Flying is like that. I suppose that almost everyone gets the opportunity to fly, at least once. But most people never do it again because they either believe that it couldn't really have happened, or they get caught by the illogicality of the whole thing and grow afraid, or they accept the experience as a novelty which, if they did it again, would no longer be novel. If a person is going to fly, I mean really fly, first he has to want to fly more than anything else in the world. Then he has to keep his eyes open for someone who knows how to fly and when he finds him he has to have the courage to ask to be taught. And the last and most important requirement of flight is that the person has to love flying. He has to love flying for flying's sake alone: for even more than the wonders that he learns and the feeling that he has while flying; every time he is on the ground he has to yearn to be up in the air again, he has to long with a longing that lifts the wings of his thoughts, and his hands and arms in supplication. If he doesn't love flying in this way then he isn't really flying; he is merely bouncing around from one place to another.

'Where was I? Oh, yeh . . . Like I said Dick must have stopped for a moment and cast a spell on me while he was coming along those old London rooftops because I was enraptured; when everybody in the movie went flying over the countryside (through a painting on a sidewalk) with the carnival carousel horses I wanted so badly to be up there with them, more than anything I had ever wanted before. I wanted it so badly that my jaw hurt.

'Later that night when everybody was asleep except me – I couldn't sleep for wanting to fly so much – it happened. I must have thought it a coincidence at the time but I know better now. I got up from my bed and looked out the window. And just who do you think was on the other side looking in? Dick was, that's who! I wasn't the least bit frightened that he was suddenly there; I suppose I had hoped so hard that he would be, that I expected him. His nose was pressed to the window pane and when I opened the window he almost went up with it. But he recovered quickly and said, "Hi. I guess you're a little surprised, huh?"

'"Nope," I said, "Will you teach me to fly too?" I was so excited that I couldn't wait, and even forgot to welcome him in. He was down on his hands and knees, crouched and leaning toward the window. My room in that house was just below ground level and the window was right on the ground if you were looking into the room. If you were looking out of the room then the window was exactly where it was supposed to be except that all you could ever see were people's feet as they walked by.

'But he wasn't about to sit there waiting for the invitation – he just crawled right in. I tried to warn him that every time I had come in that window I tumbled to the floor and hit my head on the bedstead getting up again. Every time. But it was too late because he had already started to tumble just like I always did; and that's when the first strange thing happened. He started to fall in slow motion and began to right himself – like a cat does when it falls. When he reached the floor he was sitting down just as if he always came in that way. Without hitting his head on the bed or anything.

'"Wow, how did you do that? Will you teach me to do that after you teach me to fly?"

'"That was flying. And what makes you think that I'm going to teach you how to fly anyway?" I think he was trying to scare me then, but he never was very good at scaring people; I knew that he would teach me. He had to. "How come you want to learn to fly?"

'"Cause I want to fly."

'"No," he was a little taken back, "how come you want to fly?"

'"Just because I want to. I want to really bad."

'"That's not a good enough reason. Now why?"

'I almost got angry, "Because I want to and that is too a good enough reason. Now will you teach me?"

'"Oh! It is?" He was a bit puzzled. I was to find out later that Dick was always a little bit puzzled but I suppose that was because so many strange things always happened around him. There weren't a whole lot of logical and straight-forward sequences in Dick's world. But everything that seemed to happen always turned out best for him so he was good-natured about it. Then he laughed the way he does, shaking his shoulders a bit – you know, you've seen him – and said, "OK. So let's start." Then we both climbed out the window again and he was mumbling, "Don't you have any doors in this room?"

'That first night he came to teach me was clear and moonlit so it was very pleasant for practicing take-offs and landings. Dick always emphasized style – he was very big on good style and thought that flying should be beautiful – he often told me to watch the pigeons carefully, saying that they didn't get into games or acrobatics much but that their form was excellent and very beautiful. Anyway, that night he had me practicing my first jumping. "Just jump," he said. "No, not forward but up. And then come down again softly, slowly. On the balls of your toes and then roll back to your heels as you come down into a crouch. Yeh, that's good. Bend your knees a little bit more – a real deep crouch . . . Now go up again – slowly, almost slow motion – but go higher this time. Yes, yes. Very good. You might just make a flier one day, my boy. By the way, what's your name?"

'I told him. But I always addressed him as Mr Van Dyke. At least until we were flying together pretty regularly for the pleasure of one another's company. You know, Dick is really a patient man; and I remember that first night: he and I, hand-in-hand, in the middle of a pasture just down the road from my house. We were jumping together because those first few times that you get up a little altitude – fifteen, twenty feet, say – and then look down realizing that there isn't anything there to support you except your own believing, you get mighty scared. One time we were up about twenty feet in eight or ten jumps – it takes a long time to get up when you're just a beginner or if you're in the wrong state of mind and can't shake it – and I looked down too fast. Oh God, was I scared! I was sure I was going to plummet straight down. I grabbed onto Dick's arm with both hands and must have pulled him down a good ten feet before he calmed me and led me down slowly.

'And when we landed again Dick came down with his foot in a cow pie. Lord, was he mad. He turned to me and told me very sternly to never do that again. I upset his rhythm, he said; but then he softened again and said, "Look kid, you just got to believe. That's

'*Just jump,*' *he said.* '*No, not forward but up.*'

(William Blake, 'O, How I Dreamt of Things Impossible'; Reproduced by Courtesy of the Trustees of the British Museum)

all there is to it. It's really pretty simple once you get the rhythm . . .
Now let's go up one more time and then back to your house. But
this time with no hands." So up we went again. Me first. Then he
followed, and we must have looked like two people on a trampoline
except that there wasn't a trampoline anywhere around. I remember
that night as one of the best of my life and I told Dick so too. He
really likes kids a lot but he was getting on in years even then. Those
first few weeks must have been exhausting for him. He limited me to
one day a week flying and one evening "on the ground instruction".
He wanted me to think about things and remember every moment a
good long time between every flight. I've got to admit that the
reliving it is just about as good as the flying itself. It's not difficult to
understand how some people get caught up in the remembering and
slowly stop flying altogether. But I don't think I could ever become
one of them because I love the push and the pull of the wind too
much.

'Finally after about a year or so he let me fly on my own and
whenever I felt like it. But every time I got that urge to fly really
bad, as though it were lifting me up by itself alone, Dick was always
somewhere around and he'd meet me up there and we'd fly together for a bit. When I got that real deep urge it was like a voice
inside me saying, "It's time to be up there; you've been on the
ground too long." And up and off I'd go. Then one time at the
university in Lincoln – one afternoon about four, I think – I got
that feeling and heard that call. I just went straight up; in three
bounces I was level with the roof of a six-story building and there
I saw Dick sitting with his back toward me. I recognized him
by his tweed cap that he always cocked forward toward his left
eye. So very quietly and slowly I came down behind him and
heard him saying, ". . . on the ground too long". Exactly what
I'd been hearing in my heart all those years. Then I whispered
behind him, "It's time to be up there . . ." He must have jumped
ten feet! Right to the edge of the roof and then he teetered there
a few seconds. I giggled at his predicament and then said, "Just
jump, Dick!" That was the first time I had called him by his Christian
name. But still, on occasion, I call him "Sir". He is certainly worthy
of the respect.

'"Oh yeh. I almost forgot!" and he did a backwards flip off the
edge just as if it were a diving board. When he appeared at roof level
again he said, "Boy, did you give me a scare. What were you doing

back there anyhow? I was expecting you to walk down to that field over there before you came up."

'"I just couldn't wait to be off the ground. That voice of yours is pretty powerful, you know."

'"You found out, eh?" Then he laughed in his way. "Yes, I guess it is at that. I've been practicing for a long time now. But no more."

'"Well, it's probably pretty deep inside me by now. I don't think I'll ever forget it. Come on, let's fly. You sure looked funny on that ledge a minute ago."

'We flew together as friends and equals after that . . .

'The last time we flew together was about a month before I left the States. I had been attending the university at Eureka and was becoming more and more dissatisfied, even unhappy at times; our flights together were a comfort and a relaxation. I told him about my plans to leave the country and, although he was saddened at the prospect, he agreed that it was probably the best thing. He said that he would try to arrange a visit to Africa. He did too.

'That particular day I didn't have my motorcycle with me – no gas – and since I was attending classes in Eureka while living about five miles away in one of the outlying communities I would have to hitch-hike home. I was awfully tired; however, it happened to be that time of the afternoon when the train was slowly winding its way through town. I decided to hop up onto the caboose and get a quick ride home. Watching the land close away from the back of a train is an invigorating and an inspiring thing. The train cuts a path through the trees and around the hillsides and gives a person the feeling of freedom and travel. I was refreshed by the time the train entered my little town but it did not slow down as I had expected. Instead it remained at a good clip – perhaps thirty-five miles an hour – and that was where I had to get off! First I threw my knapsack of books off, then asked myself why I had done that because now I really had no choice, and finally I jumped. Rocks seemed to hit me from everywhere at once and I rolled over once or twice but I got up with only a small scrape on one arm and what felt like a cut on my leg. I looked and there was a short rip in my pants and so probably a little skin torn too. But it felt good! It's important to do things like jumping off trains once in a while – something that I had often seen on the television and had always wanted to do myself. Now I had done it. I was elated. Torn clothes and a few bruises were a small price to pay for the experience. The tear in the pants I could sew that night – the wrong color thread, of course – but it could easily be mended and washed by morning.

'I was so happy I could fly. I began bouncing, and bounced myself up the street, over the trees, and around to my house. And there, to my surprise and joy, was Dick sitting in a barber's chair in my neighbor's front yard getting a shave. It looked as though the neighbors had taken up a new business because there were four or five people waiting in line after Dick. Funny business, I thought, for a front yard.

'I went upstairs to my room and put my books away and then bounded out of my window and was back at the neighbors just as Dick heaved himself up out of the chair. As I came up I asked him, "How are we going to go anywhere if you're feeling too heavy to get out of a barber's chair?" And someone put in, "Putting on weight, Dick?"

'"You're only as heavy as you feel", he said and went on, "I was going to ask you the same question exactly. I saw you in Eureka not an hour ago and you looked as if the whole world was pressing you down."

'"An hour ago it was. Bad classes, a hard day: same old story. But I don't even want to think about it. I'm feeling in a flying mood now . . . just had an exciting train ride."

'"That was you, was it? Well, you're full of surprises. One of the boys here was just saying that he saw a youngster jump off that train that just whistled by. From what he said, your form was good. Uhh . . . yes, 'Devil may care' I think he said. Not bad at all, my boy."

'"Thank you, Sir. How you feeling now? Like a quick trip into the hills?"

'"Yeh, sounds good to me. Let's take it slow and easy. And say, there's someone we can pick up. Someone I think you'll enjoy meeting."

'We flew back into Eureka and came down on the south side of the tracks. Dick walked across a street to a small shingle-board house and knocked at the door. A little girl about twelve or thirteen opened it and then jumped right at Dick. "Señor, oh, I am so happy to see you!" She was pretty, dark-eyed, full of smiles and her hands full of charcoal – from cleaning, I suppose. "Oh! Pardón, Señor." She wiped her hands on her apron leaving a deep black smudge on either side. Dick wiped the back of his neck with his handkerchief but was grinning all the while.

'"Maria, Adam is in the field waiting. We are going into the hills for a couple of hours before sunset. Do you want to go?"

'"Oh, yes, yes, Señor. Let me tell mama. MAMA . . ." she disappeared into the back rooms and reappeared again in trousers and a shirt. She and Dick ambled back over to where I sat in the field. Maria suddenly became real shy the way young girls do and when Dick introduced her as Anna Maria Lopez and me by my first name alone, she curtsied a little and said "Thank you, Sir."

'I laughed in reply, "I'm not Sir; he's Sir," pointing to Dick, "I'm just Adam."

'She flushed and said, "Oh!" then brightened, "That's only my short name too. But if I tell you all my names we could stand here until the sun is gone. You call me Maria", and she laughed.

'"Good. Are you ready to go?" She nodded and I turned to Dick, "Ready?"

'"We're off," and he was. As we flew Dick told me to take it easy because this was only Maria's second trip. She had been flying with Dick for a little over two months at that time. When we found a pleasant meadow, surrounded by trees, on the west side of a hill, we landed. That is, Dick and I landed. Maria was bubbling with excitement and while Dick and I stretched out on the grass she bounced over the trees and practiced recovery from rolls and the regulation of speed.

'"She's pretty excited by it all. And it looks like she'll be a good flier."

'"No different from the way you were ten years ago. But, given time, she might just be better than you or me. If you keep your ears open, you're going to hear of her again one day. There's an awful lot of potential behind those pretty black eyes. But then, I only pick the best," he said, nudging me with his elbow.

'"Did you ever think that it was us who picked the best?" I returned. He laughed it off; he was really a very humble man. But then I guess humility and nobility go hand-in-hand.

'That was our last conversation together except for his brief visit to Africa. That first movie – *Mary Poppins* – was playing for a few weeks in Dar es Salaam not long before I left Tanzania. I sat through it three times and each time it was as if Dick were sitting beside me and showing me the wonder of things all over again. Who knows? Maybe he was.'

When Adam's family all lived together in the white house on the hill in Massachusetts a strange thing happened. It was a sensation, a vision, which he was to treasure all his life. On that hill one autumn afternoon it occurred for the first time, the best time.

The white house on the hill off Maynard Road was quaint and picturesque. Two weeks before this incident the house could barely be seen through the flush of color that the birch and elm trees gloriously paraded. Now, however, the leaves had begun to drift down into a carpet on the grass leaving the trees naked to face the coming winter winds. The crest of the hill was spacious, particularly to a boy of eleven: there was the house itself and what must have seemed like an acre of trees and ground seeded with grass. The upkeep of the yard was Adam's responsibility and he often thought of the land as his own. He loved the birch trees more than the others because they were so different. Unique difference would always attract Adam. He had read that the local Indians had, long ago, used birch to make their canoes. Perhaps they had loved that difference also. But now all the Indians were dead and forgotten. The land never remembered who hunted on it and the rivers never said who had fished in them. But the birch trees still held some faint memory and they allowed Adam to make it flesh. It saddened him that the trees should lose their beautiful coats, that they were abandoned in the hour of their greatest need.

Adam raked the leaves into great piles which he and Barbara would jump and roll about in until they were exhausted and the piles smashed flat. Though it was still early, and the leaves would continue to fall where Adam was now raking, making the obligation twofold, he was happy to be a part of the leaves and the trees and the land. In acts of love, obligations twice performed are many times better. There was naught but the savor of love and joy about his work.

As Adam raked he slowly became filled with a sensation of speed. It overtook him gradually: beginning as a low buzz, it slowly and evenly heightened to a high-pitched hum. His body and limbs conformed to the sound and he began to move more rapidly around the pile; the movement of his arms accelerated accordingly. With the hum and the sensation of speed came an awareness of distance as though they were not Adam's own arms deftly swishing the rake or his own legs scurrying about. Then, as if these three diverse phenomena focused on a single point, Adam realized what had happened. With his eyes he saw himself, below the place where he was, furiously raking leaves. The hum and the speed settled into a vibration of his entire being – that being divorced from the one below who continued to work. Adam was above in vibrant rest; he floated, attached to himself by the merest silver cord. Perhaps it was the cord that he had come through with such speed and sound.

Adam did not remember returning but next he knew he was leaning and holding tightly onto the rake. The vibration still filled him and he lay down in the leaves to fully appreciate the sensation. He lay there absorbing it until it subsided; but it didn't really, it seemed to flutter away to where it had come from. Adam slowly arose leaving the rake behind him and went directly to his bedroom, speaking to no one as he passed, and there he lay down again on his back so that he would not forget.

The experience occurred two or three times during the year on the hill. It was each time the same, although the situation differed. He was walking on the sidewalk downtown one sunny afternoon and the buildings were tall around him. Then he was walking faster and faster and again suddenly he was only watching himself walk. But, although he was not moving in the least above, while below he walked on, still he was always in the same position above and to one side of himself, tied by the silver cord through which he must have passed. Just as the passage of space could not be recognized or measured, so too it was with the passage of time. Was he outside of himself for the seconds it seemed, or for minutes, or for less than an instant? Adam did not and could not know. Neither was this in any way similar to flying. Adam had been flying for some time and he knew the difference: flying was in time and space; this involved neither, but was in some way a completely different reality.

There were only the three or four different situations that Adam could recall. But they all occurred within the year and never clearly and distinctly in an awakened state after that time. It often happened that Adam would be sleeping when he seemed to relive the experience in its entirety, most usually in the situation of raking leaves. Adam cultivated these dreams and absorbed them completely, years after the situations themselves had passed. There was always some part of Adam that waited – waited patiently – until the sound or the speed again appeared, even if it were only faintly discernible. Then that part of him was immediately alive. It was in control, welcoming the experience as a host might welcome a loved guest.

Today Adam sleeps very deeply and seldom remembers his dreams. He journeys both day and night but no longer charts the journeys himself. Perhaps they are unchartable. But still, on occasion, he will awake experiencing the vibration of every cell and part. He lies quietly, contentedly, and enjoys the reverberations of another world until slowly they become a flutter and flutter out of him leaving him in this world to perform this world's obligations once again.

CHAPTER IV

Being how Adam first realizes his discontent and
restlessly defines his journey

And Joseph went after his brethren, and found them in Dothan. And when they saw him afar off, even before he came near unto them, they conspired against him to slay him. And they said one unto another, Behold, this dreamer cometh. Come now therefore, and let us slay him, and cast him into some pit, and we will say, Some evil beast hath devoured him: and we shall see what will become of his dreams . . . and Judah said unto his brethren, What profit is it if we slay our brother, and conceal his blood? Come, and let us sell him to the Ishmaelites, and let not our hand be upon him; for he is our brother and our flesh. And his brethren were content.

Genesis 37:17–27

I

Adam's mother had always maintained that her first-born was a difficult child right from the start. Other children could be appeased and would be content; Adam could not and would not be. He was a test and a trial from the moment of his conception. Adam's mother first realized she was pregnant when Adam, dissatisfied with his living quarters, began to rearrange them. 'My God,' she would say later, 'was I sick!'

Even though in her social conversations she joked about it being something less than human which she had conceived, she did not know how very right she was: it was something struggling to become human. The station of man is inestimably high, but it is not one bestowed unconditionally: it must be gained through constant endeavor. Adam was aware of this condition immediately and wasted no time in beginning his climb. If he wasn't moving he wasn't happy. But then, his unhappiness would force him to move again. Unhappiness is a gift and Adam accepted it as such. Such things are, however, very difficult for a mother to understand and so she naturally misapplies consoling for compassion. When Adam spoke about his childhood, he spoke about his unhappiness, but never disparagingly. He would say he was glad that it had happened but he was also glad it was over. It was very hard on everyone involved.

For the longest time Adam could not understand why he had been given such obviously inadequate quarters. Surely there were better available? He spent his first months rearranging them, first one way and then another; Adam's mother was constantly sick. When there seemed no more room to rearrange them he kicked and pushed the collapsing walls back. Then suddenly there was a lurching, and again, and again; Adam was pushed through an all-too-narrow passage. The lurching, he had to admit, was disconcerting at the least. But he was moving and that was satisfying. The kicking and pushing had paid off – perhaps he was moving to better quarters. It was recorded as one of the shortest labors in that hospital, so anxious was Adam to be free.

Suddenly there was light and enough space to satisfy even Adam. It was a new world, a glorious world. He was free. He could not have imagined such a paradise. But that was just what it was: his imagination running wild. He was soon made painfully aware of reality. There were other creatures in this new world and although Adam could not distinguish them from the world itself, he could feel their presence. The creatures were busy, very busy about something, and in their busy-ness they forgot their manners; one of them was full of hostility and had the audacity to vent his problem on Adam. Adam cried out and the hostile one seemed satisfied. Perhaps he thought he had inflicted some small pain. But Adam had not cried because of any hurt inflicted by that hostility. That would be foolish. How, after being in constant pain all of his life, could Adam even consider such a mild provocation? No, his pain was much deeper. That person's hostility had only served to awaken him from his imagining and it was this awakening that was so very painful. It was the sudden awareness that even in this glorious new world of light and independence he was not free. Instead he was cast into an insignificant form that, to all appearances, he was helpless to control. 'O God,' he cried, 'why hast Thou forsaken me?' His quarters had not changed at all. The day had dawned and Adam had been given knowledge and sight; but not liberty. He must still learn his liberty. With the dawning of understanding he saw his quarters clearly in their true light. He was in a prison.

At first Adam was mad, damn mad. He howled for days on end. He howled at anybody who would listen; but nobody listened long. So when left alone he howled himself to sleep. At least, if he wasn't free when he was asleep, he wasn't imprisoned either. To see Adam sleeping one would have thought him an angel; but no one said so too loudly or Adam would begin to howl and one would wonder what he was. He was a *discontent*.

It did not take Adam long to realize that howling was getting him nowhere; and besides, it was too time-consuming and the noise too loud, especially in small rooms where the sound reverberated off the walls. There had to be another way. Adam became suddenly quiet and watchful (to everyone's relief). He became aware that there were certain expectations and responsibilities asked of him: expectations like feeding, responsibilities like smiling. He thought that perhaps through these things he would find a way out of his prison. He tried to do everything he was supposed to. He watched everything and everyone closely and tried to understand the mysteries of this world. There were so many mysteries, so many un-understandable phenomena. Slowly, gradually he began to make connections and establish patterns, and to understand the workings of this – his – world. There were wonders at every moment and a host of emotions: from excitement to despair; there were heights and depths and Adam could learn from them all. But never did Adam forget the reason why he learned.

2

To say that the world was wonderful, as Adam often did, was to say that it was full of wonder. Adam was tossed on seas of wonder; surrounded and enveloped by things so much larger and greater than himself.

Wondering is learning taken beyond its moderate form. Wonder was natural to Adam, who took everything to its extremity that he might understand its implications. Adam would often lie for long hours on the grass in the warmth of the sun or the cool of the shade, or again he would lie on his bed at night and long hours passed quickly until sleep finally overcame him. There was so much to wonder about.

Wondering is easily distinguished from thinking by its posture alone. A person sits when he is thinking, often holding his head; but when he wonders he is lying prostrate and his head is holding the world. Adam lay on his belly and wondered about the earth; he lay on his back and wondered about the heavens.

When Adam was five years old he took possession of five square feet of land between the side of the house and the sidewalk that led to the back yard. He dug up this little parcel of land and carefully prepared it for the carrot seeds which had been bought for him. He planted the carrot seeds and a wonderful thing happened. Carrots grew. Adam would lie on the grass, near where his land was magically forming green-topped carrots from the seeds he had offered it, and wonder about this thing. The carrots grew, and Adam grew, and the world grew wider and more wonderful.

Then one day a little boy who was Adam's friend came and saw Adam wondering and he saw the carrot-growing that Adam was wondering about. But he did not stop and lie down and wonder about them too; he thought about them. What he thought about them was that they should be pulled up and eaten so that Adam could come and play. So he did.

Adam was very angry and the little boy was very surprised. He was no longer Adam's friend because Adam beat him up. Adam was very angry indeed! Maybe being beaten up taught the little boy to wonder about carrot-growing and not to think about it. The incident also gave Adam something new to wonder about. He wondered about cruelty, stupidity, anger and violence. But most of all he wondered about these things within himself. The earth taught Adam to wonder about himself.

A person can lie on his belly and wonder, but by far the most comfortable position to wonder in is, of course, lying on his back. But not all times are fit to lie on one's back and wonder. The heavens must be in a particularly auspicious mood, that wonder be inspired. And make no mistake about it, the heavens do have moods. During the day a person should only wonder about the heavens if they are overcast or if there are clouds scampering past.

It is the clouds, always busy going somewhere and doing something, that make the day sky wonderful. Their shifting patterns and forms, their unknown destinations, the endless possibilities, develop the imagination – a child's most important tool. With his imagination Adam often climbed right up into those clouds and explored their most hidden insides. He explored for ancient castles, for misty ships, and sometimes for great monsters hidden in caves which he could vanquish. Sometimes Adam used his imagination as a halter and guided a bucking, resisting cloud the way he wanted to go. Mere clouds were helpless before Adam's imagination. But by far the best thing about clouds was that they were always coming from and going to distant and exciting lands. They would absorb evaporating rivers in one land and send down their raindrops in another. Adam knew the clouds were messengers with stories to tell about new and strange places; he never let a cloud pass before it had told all it had to tell. Oh, clouds were wonderful things! They could tell not only about distant places, but, because they were always coming from yesterday and going to tomorrow they could also tell about distant times. Adam often heard stories of his own future from the clouds and he wondered about these stories.

During the night a person should only wonder about the heavens if it is clear and the stars are out. Oh, it is true that overcast nights during the full moon are full of wonder, but because of the rarity of such nights, the similarity to day-sky wondering, and simply for convenience' sake, these are best classified as part and parcel of that mentioned above. Night-sky wondering is a unique and wholly different brand of wondering. When Adam was able to be outside at these late hours or when the night sky was so brilliant and inviting that he could wonder about it through the window of his darkened bedroom he leapt out far, far beyond our puny affairs. Our affairs were surely unnoticed in the midst of such overwhelming vastness. Yet they received so much attention. Our world was both so big and so small at one and the same time. We were, after all, important in our own eyes and, for all that we were told, in God's eyes too. Amongst these unnumbered stars attention was lavished upon our little earth like it is upon a newborn babe. We were held tightly in the arms of the Great Mother; something to wonder about, surely.

Further, there were so many stars. Stars were like people: they were uncountable; and they were constantly being born and dying. Surely there must be a star for every person on the earth, their own personal star that was in some unexplainable way connected only to them. It appeared when they were born – like the Bethlehem Star – and disappeared when they died. It led them, and guided them as a guardian angel might, and it was their destiny. If they grew to genius then it descended upon them. That was what falling stars were: the bestowal of genius. Adam wondered about this. He wondered if he was destined for genius, if his star would descend. The heavens taught Adam to wonder about himself.

There is a great power in wonder. A child becomes great when he wonders about great things. When he wonders he goes far beyond himself and deep into himself, for the universe is folded up within him. Wonder is a child's work and is worthy of his hours. When he wonders he becomes tomorrow, and truly a child. He is becoming man.

3

The wonders of the world directed Adam inward and caused him to ponder his own nature and reality. This was natural. Other aspects of the world – less natural aspects – also caused him to turn inward.

From the moment of his birth he began to realize that this was a violent place and that the world's creatures indulged their hostilities and angers with a vengeance. The doctor's hostility toward Adam on the night of his birth served as a warning of what was to come.

A young child's world is cruel and unpredictable. Its very un-predictability is a cruelty. Adam was an energetic child and one whose whole life, from its first beginnings, was of searching, of learning new things; he was propelled toward seeking some un-definable, unattainable something. His hands were in everything, his eyes saw everything and his tongue asked questions about every-thing he saw. He was a nuisance! Many times he would do something in his daily quest for understanding (like reaching for the paint can on the top shelf in the garage) only to be told, bluntly and harshly, that it was wrong or bad or dangerous. If he reached for something his hand was slapped. If he built something he found out that he should not have used the materials he had. If he tasted something he was scolded because it was to be saved. 'For what?' Adam asked, and he was scorned. 'Saved just to be saved', he realized. One day he ate something and everyone turned very cruel. They took him to a doctor to pump it out of his stomach. What a horrible experience! But Adam learned.

If he spoke to someone who reacted harshly then he turned away and did not try to speak to him again. If he could not turn away physically because it was impolite – he was taught to be polite to everyone – then he turned away mentally. The harsh and violent nature of the people he met caused him to separate himself from them and live his life from within. He learned not to love anything or anyone overmuch. He was divorced from the things and the people around him.

This great divorce was Adam's only protection: an armor like that defenseless animals make for themselves. He became distant from his family and acquaintances. They thought he was cold, unloving, silent. He was wary. If he was unloving, he was not cruel: his silence and his distance might unsettle people a bit or puzzle them but it did not inflict a hurt upon them.

Adam could not hurt other people or other creatures because he felt their pain, a pain that was sharp and poignant. He merely watched from a distance with big, pitying eyes. Once, much later in his life, he was hitch-hiking in France and the day was not going well. No one was kind; everyone was afraid or in a hurry. He had somewhere to go but he was not getting there. As he paced back and forth along the side of the road he grew angry at the people's unhelpful attitude. Suddenly, he drew his foot back and kicked hard and hatefully at a group of yellow dandelions that were peacefully enjoying the warmth of the sun. Their heads popped off and their stems fell broken and twisted to the ground. The pain of it struck him so hard that he was almost knocked to the ground himself. If it had been in his power he would have carefully straightened every stem and lovingly replaced every head. But he could not do this: he could only think of the pain inflicted by his own cruelty.

The hurt, the pain, the cruelty, the anger of the world caused Adam to turn away from it. He turned to learning. He learned about his own potential and changed his own nature through his interaction with the world. When, in some childish prank that ended wrong, he caused someone to be saddened he could not forget it for days. Over the years Adam produced a great repertoire of such incidents and they inhabited a corner of his mind. The slightest suggestion of some action similar to one he stored, and which he knew only ended in hurt, checked him in mid-step or mid-speech. He seldom made the same mistake twice. He was both a quick learner and a strict, even harsh, master. Although kept from repeating old mistakes, thereby giving him the time and opportunity to make new ones, he was haunted by the review of them: there was always some part of his mind that was ever living old horror stories of foolishness and nightmares – his own horror stories of foolishness and nightmares of cruelty.

Not only did Adam have the results and effect of actions played reel-to-reel in living color in that unique piece of machinery that sat on his shoulders, but he also saw flashing warnings of patterns and sequences. One morning, for example, he was walking from a large department store with his father when loud noises in the parking lot attracted his attention and caused him to stop. Two men, thirty feet from each other and each only half out of his car, were shouting and hurling curses at one another. There was hatred in their words, and threats in their actions. As Adam listened and watched he somehow became aware that there would be a third world war. It was not a thought or a possibility; it was a solid knowledge which he could not explain, but which these two men taught him. Adam never accepted anything at its face value but saw each action or word as though it were spiraling forward or backward in a time tunnel of concentric circles, and whirling along beside it were its implications and possibilities. He saw many great and many terrible truths.

Through these forests of recorded mistakes and these craggy badlands of visions and implications Adam had to choose a path. Slowly, bit by bit and step by step he did this: carefully, but daily, he cast brambles out of his way and he cut entangling vines and creepers. One day Adam would discover that it was a road he had been clearing all along.

4

The course of Adam's learning, though occasionally fantastic, was never fantasy. He never used his imagination to create other worlds where all things were good. But he did, in a sense, create another being of himself to live in this world. He never tried to escape the reality of this world, but in his seeking to understand it, it changed before his eyes. He learned that the way he saw reality was the way it was.

The night is an example. Adam, as a young child, often heard that night was a frightening time: a time when a child can't see and doesn't know who or what might be near him; a time when common sounds take on an eerie aspect, surrounding and confusing him; a time when things grow pointed and longer and bigger than they should be, and as they grow bigger they also grow more aggressive, waiting in their dark corners to attack. But Adam did not believe these things because adults did not seem particularly frightened by the dark of night. If they had some chore that was as yet unfinished by nightfall, then as often as not they would rise after the evening meal and go out into the darkness and finish it. A heavier coat was all the protection they felt they needed.

Adam went out into the night as often as he could and for as long as he could. At night everything was muted and less harsh. The sun never blinded him and yet there was always just enough light to see the outlines of things that needed to be seen. From the first, Adam learned that on leaving a lighted house, if he stood silently and waited, the sudden darkness that had enveloped him would begin to part and small lights would come forward to give the night a gray mistiness.

The night was most like a friend because it enticed Adam to conversation. He could go and walk around the yard or into the group of nearby trees and hold complete dialogues. He spoke to the night about things which most people thought were silly or which they had made clear they did not like to talk about. These things were important to Adam and they needed to be talked out. The night let him do this.

As Adam walked and talked he did not have to wait for the night to respond. Night was a very mystical friend because through its silence he could distinctly hear a response within his own heart. Nor was he afraid with his friend to give voice to these answers to see if they sounded as right (or as wrong) as they felt. The night could be trusted with secrets: it never told to anyone what they had spoken of. Even when they argued, and Adam waved his arms about thrashing the air, the night hid him from the mirth or pity of others until the clash yielded a truth or a peace. Night's reality, Adam saw, was that of a true friend and not a feared enemy. It was with these eyes that he looked out upon the world. This was his secret elixir that changed the world.

5

The world taught Adam about itself from within himself. It showed him its chains and tangling vines and it showed him its wonders; it showed him its meanness and its beauty. It showed Adam how to think about it, and how to see it, and how to change it by seeing it differently. The world taught him the use of its instruments and tools as a knight teaches his squire the use of armor and weapons. Like the squire who trusts his master, Adam trusted that which taught him; he never misused the weapons or ran away seeking adventures before he was prepared and ready. But once prepared, the mover in him did not allow him to stay back in a place of ease either. Having the power of knowledge in one hand and the weapon of sight in the other, he began to understand the quest before him and he was drawn into it.

Perhaps Adam was another Don Quixote set out to fight windmills and disguised demons that others did not recognize. Not being able to see, they did not know of the dangers that threatened them. But Adam saw the demons as well as the old Don himself; and in the fight he gave them no quarter. Equally important, accepted none from them. He would not have peace in these matters through compromise; but Adam never would, never could compromise in battle. He was not a shopkeeper seeking a peaceful atmosphere in which to transact business, nor was he a banker set upon a regular course. He was a hero and was not satisfied unless his world was spinning.

He did not have to travel far before he discovered his windmills, his ugly giants who imprisoned the people. He sought the mistress of compassion and understanding but in her place pity reared its head. He sought the maid who balances justice in her scales but found only a withered and embittered old hag dealing in injustice. He sought love and found usury; independence and found sulking, crippled imitation; beauty and found only its reflection. Adam prepared for siege: he had set out to attack and found himself besieged on all fronts.

Adam was, as I have shown, not like most other children. His thoughts and inclinations were not like those of other children; his motives and actions were not those of other children. This caused him to seek compassion and understanding somehow knowing that it would make both him and the ones who understood that little bit stronger. But children are cruel and laugh at what is different. No one was made stronger by their laughter. His father could not understand because by nature fathers do not understand their sons, that the world may progress. Adam's mother wanted to understand, but a mother's wanting is seldom pure. She needed to comfort him more than she wanted to understand and so was unable to do either. Finally Adam, through realizing the rarity of true compassion, cut off pity's ugly head and sadly admitted his first victory.

Because he was not understood, he seldom saw justice dispensed in his behalf. His family once had neighbors who had a lovely and fruitful garden. Late one autumn these neighbors took a short holiday and left no one to care for their house and garden. Adam was fond of these people and when he was passing the garden one day he saw that the leaves had fallen heavily covering it. It did not occur to him that there were few trees in that immediate area and that the leaves could not have naturally piled up there. He knew that, where there were leaves, there it needed raking. So to surprise his neighbors upon their return he raked the garden clear and left the leaves in great piles by its side. The neighbors were surprised but it was not the joyful surprise that Adam had expected; it was angry surprise. At this sudden development Adam became silent: his joy in serving became a guilt for damaging. The neighbors found out that Adam was the criminal (and now he felt and acted like one too) and next he knew he was standing, listening as his neighbor complained to his mother against him. 'Give him an inch and he takes a yard', she said. Had Adam only been able to explain! He would have raked all the leaves back into the garden, where, he found, they were supposed to be for the winter, if only he were given the chance. After all, he had meant to help, not harm. But he was not given the chance. Not justice, but embittered injustice was dispensed. Adam learned, however: not only about gardens in wintertime, but also about service and surprises and, most important, about how very rapidly things can change. Adam grew to understand that his learning these things was justice. There was justice in injustice itself. It was another victory – a victory through seeing. Slowly Adam grew to judge things fairly, but he never cried if they were not so judged by others.

During these years Adam had no friends; this was not because he was unfriendly but because he did not make the pacts of friendship that most boys do. He was wary because, as he watched other boys, he discovered that they did not choose their friends for love as he thought was right, but for convenience and advantage. There were all kinds of social intricacies and puzzles that made one person's friendship more valuable than another's. He tried to understand these things but they were ultimately beyond him. He honestly wondered if anyone really understood these phantom social orders or if people just pretended to. At any rate he could not allow himself to be used in this manner; if anyone approached him with anything less than absolute sincerity he turned away as he would from one who carried the plague. Realizing that the love of another for that other's sake alone rather than for one's own sake was unknown, and that friends would be few at the best of times, was another step on the journey.

When Adam sought independence of thought and action amongst a people said to be the most independent in the world, he found only imitation and a cringing fear of being thought fundamentally different from the majority. These people who prided themselves on their freedom only thought exactly what the newspapers told them to think! The opposite point of view was beyond their imagination. If they heard it, they laughed it out of existence. Could it be possible that the Chinese were not a secretive yellow army, a billion strong, who sought nothing but the embarrassment of all Americans? Or that, beneath all the propaganda and hatred and fear, the communist was human too? – that in the final analysis he and the democrat sought fundamentally the same ends? No, to the average imitative mind, these things were not possible. Adam discovered that people really did not want to think for themselves: let the politicians be responsible for their lives, the newspapers responsible for their thoughts, and the priest or the television preacher responsible for their souls and their God. Let them, they said, conduct their business in peace. Adam could not abide this; of anything that he saw or was told he was as inclined to believe its opposite as he was to believe it itself. Often he admitted both. Another idol lay crashed and broken at his feet. Still the journey continued; if anything, the road grew longer rather than shorter.

Beauty set itself before Adam because, as he passed through adolescence – a time when beauty is a very important social asset – he was ugly. His face turned red and blotched with pimples. Rare was the morning during those five years, that, upon looking in the mirror, he would count less than fifteen of the oily, seething sores on his cheeks, chin and forehead. He flushed at the very mention of the word 'pimple' and longed for the time when he would have a beard to cover his ugly cheeks and chin. But for all this, he knew that inside he was not ugly, that there was a beauty in his soul that longed to be appreciated. In his search after beauty he began to look deep within others' eyes rather than at some more superficial part. Nor was it long before he discovered a secret connection between those who suffered ridicule because of their ugly faces or their poor clothes, and beauty itself. It was deepset in these people's eyes – though sometimes they themselves did not know it – but rarely in the eyes of those thought beautiful. Society ignored a great truth and lost something precious by its ignorance.

Beauty was how Adam last defined his quest, but when he found it in its secret place, his journey had not come to an end. He had fully realized by then that the final object of his search, his journey's goal, was beyond definition or declaration. He continued on the path that ever opened before him, but his goal was unknowable. Adam grew to accept it that way. If he did not name it, he did not limit it. Neither was he afraid that he would not recognize it at the journey's end – that was, if the journey ended. And Adam had begun to think that it might never end at all.

6

Adam was born a son amongst the blessed upon the earth. He was born in that western land that produced conquerors and men of arms, wizards and men of knowledge, giants and men of industry. But he was the third son, the disinherited: a recluse, and an outcast; and he could not abide the blessing until he understood it and felt himself worthy.

By his sixteenth year Adam's journey had grown to be the better part of him; his search was his constant companion. In the summer of that year he had taken a job as a cook at a pizza parlor in Eureka and often worked late into the night. He had no means of transportation then but learned to use his thumb fairly successfully. If it was too late and there were no cars on the road, then he walked the five miles between his job and his bed. He knew every inch of the road – its grades, its curves, its deserted sawmills and its railroad crossings – like he knew himself. Sometimes, as he walked, he would argue with a God whom he wasn't even sure existed, sometimes he would curse the rain and sometimes he would rejoice in it, sometimes he would lie down by the side of the road for an hour or more. It was a long walk. The next night, Adam knew, he would be walking again and he often wondered if he was really going anywhere with all this walking. He thought that perhaps if he simply stopped in one place and rested for twenty-four hours, he could pick up his routine on the following night and nothing would be lost. But he never actually did this: there was something within him goading him to walk the road every night.

After one such weary trek he arrived at his parents' house at three o'clock in the morning. He went directly to his bedroom but was filled with that active exhaustion that allows a person neither rest nor movement. He did not turn on the light in the room but raised the bamboo curtain instead. The starlight streamed in its thousand silent slivers. 'Surely starlight is the best kind of light at this hour,' Adam thought aloud.

As he sat at his desk before the wide picture window and gazed at the valley he had just walked through he saw the flicker of infrequent lights through the descending mist. The land-lights and the starlights blurred at their meeting place and in themselves; each one seemed to shoot slivers at the others as Adam's eyes lost their focus and found it again. The valley was long and the lights went on indefinitely. It became for Adam that the lights, no longer distinguishable between those that came from the distant houses and those that came from the distant stars, formed a path and lighted a way. The way had no goal and no end and seemed to lengthen as Adam tried to discern its conclusion. He realized that the way's horizons would always be beyond his ability to reach, that they would unfold before him. Then again, there came the distinct impression that he was the ever-widening horizon itself: that he, if he chose this starway, would expand as his horizons expanded, expand as a lotus does when it reaches out of an ugly water toward the beckoning sun.

Adam was suddenly and fully awake and alert with this vision; the path did not vanish as his eyes widened. The path could never vanish because Adam was on it and a part of it. Even in the most dreary mists and fogs he knew that he could be assured of the path before him – the unending, unlimited path – that went far, far beyond his ability to chart.

Perhaps another, on seeing this path, would not recognize it, or, recognizing it, would not claim it as his own. But Adam could not be any other than he always was. This path was his, he knew. He stepped forth onto it and never turned back. On that night his soul was confirmed.

CHAPTER V

*Being how greed and lust and power become
important to Adam, and how they lose their importance*

And Joseph was brought down to Egypt; and Potiphar, an officer
of Pharaoh, captain of the guard, an Egyptian, bought him of the
hands of the Ishmaelites, which had brought him down thither.
And the Lord was with Joseph and he was a prosperous man; and he
was in the house of his master the Egyptian . . .

And it came to pass after these things, that his master's wife cast
her eyes upon Joseph; and she said, Lie with me. But he refused, and
said unto his master's wife, Behold, my master wotteth not what is
with me in the house, and he hath committed all that he hath to my
hand; There is none greater in this house than I; neither hath he kept
back any thing from me but thee, because thou art his wife: how
then can I do this great wickedness, and sin against God? . . . And it
came to pass about this time, that Joseph went into the house to do
his business; and there was none of the men of the house there
within. And she caught him by his garment, saying, Lie with me:
and he left his garment in her hand, and fled, and got him out. And it
came to pass, when she saw that he had left his garment in her hand,
and was fled forth, that she called unto the men of her house, and
spake unto them, saying, See, he hath brought in an Hebrew unto
us to mock us; he came in unto me to lie with me, and I cried with a
loud voice: And it came to pass, as I lifted up my voice and cried,
that he left his garment with me, and fled, and got him out. And she
laid up his garment by her, until his lord came home . . . And it came
to pass, when his master heard the words of his wife, which she
spake unto him, saying, After this manner did thy servant to me;
that his wrath was kindled. And Joseph's master took him, and put
him into the prison, a place where the king's prisoners were bound:
and he was there in the prison.

But the Lord was with Joseph, and shewed him mercy . . .

Genesis 39:1–9, 11–21

A wise man either turns toward the world or turns away from it; only the fool is found hesitating. If a man turns toward the world it is because he is first attracted, then enticed, and at last entrapped by its charms. If he turns away, he must either naturally despise or learn to ignore these charms. It is rare that a man, having an amount of gold, does not hunger for more. It is rare that a man, on seeing a beautiful woman, does not try to engage her in conversation. It is rare that a man, having even limited influence over others, does not try to use it.

Adam was not ignorant, nor was he plagued with hesitation or doubt. But in turning toward the world he saw through its enticement and turned away again before he was entrapped by those charms that first sparkle like a wave in the sun and then enwrap and drown the unwary. He grew to become one of those who despised the lure of gold coin, ignored the half-hidden eyes of beautiful women, and distrusted influence. Still, these are not things cast once behind a person's back and quickly forgotten; they must be repeatedly shaken off his shoulders.

Adam was raised to respect the potential of money. From the age when he became aware of its existence he always had some in his pocket. His parents gave him chores and attracted his cooperation by giving him enough money for candy or, if he saved it, the book he wanted. He earned money for keeping up the yard, for taking out the trash and for assorted odd jobs which he, as often as not, solicited himself. He remembers how he and his sister would stand on chairs – because they were still too small to reach the sink comfortably – and wash and dry the dinner dishes for a nickel apiece. The nickels and quarters that were owed Adam taught him his accounting and math. Numbers and the things that numbers could do, like nickels and the things that nickels could do, never posed him any great difficulty. Indeed, he grew very comfortable and at ease in their realm.

Perhaps he grew too comfortable with them because it was not too many years before he was manipulating them to his advantage. An example of this, which he would never forget because of its intense satisfaction, involved his marks at school. The satisfaction arose from his completely rejecting common expectations, his outwitting his parents and his so successfully scorning school.

Adam and his sister received their report cards from school on a quarterly basis; their parents wanted them to succeed at things (which, at their age, meant school) and so encouraged them as they thought best. But Adam was uninspired and generally bored by school; all he had to do was not be stupid and he was moderately successful. Being successful at something he despised so never touched his fancy – he merely played the game so that no one would complain overly. Then something occurred that truly challenged him: his parents decided that an appropriate encouragement would be to pay the children a token amount for the grades they received. A rate was decided upon that generally ran as such: there would be a dime for every 'A' and a quarter for every mark raised one full grade. This last meant that a 'C' becoming a 'B' received a quarter; an 'A–' becoming an 'A' or an 'A+' received only a dime because it had not been – in this case, could not have been – raised a full grade. It did not pay to get 'A's! Immediately upon hearing of this new plan Adam retired to his room, took pencil and paper, and with the heart of a true businessman proceeded to calculate how he could make the most money out of this system without appearing to be doing so. Obviously the straightforward way would be to start with 'C's throughout ('D's would raise too much of an uproar) and gradually bring them up to 'A's. But this would be too obvious; Adam had to be subtle if this game was going to be played. Finally, after much calculation and decision about the highest permissible risk (surely he had promise as an insurance company executive) he had a game plan. It made school much more interesting: now, rather than simply doing what he was asked and later discovering it was graded as a high 'B' or a low 'A' – how very dull this had grown! – he would carefully choose his answers so that the correct percentage would be wrong and that ultimately he would get the exact mark he needed for that prized quarter. With a little practice he grew able to choose his grade within two or three percentage points. To his parents' puzzled surprise Adam's grades always went up and he always collected an optimum amount at the assessment sessions, but there never seemed to be any great improvement. He did, however, have brighter eyes when school was mentioned and this, they thought, was worth their efforts.

Money is not the root of all evil as is commonly misstated, but greed for money is certainly the root of much evil. Rare is the one who discovers money and yet is not touched by the fever of greed.

People who conduct business sooner or later discover a trace of a businessman's heart within their breast. A businessman, if he is to be successful, must not only be completely comfortable and at ease with accounts, but he must also be fully cognizant of people's tastes. A businessman's heart considers well people's tastes, but seldom their needs.

Adam wanted a little more money to support a taste that he had developed and so to do this he made himself aware of other people's tastes. When he was fourteen he came upon an interesting little business venture that would supply him the cash he needed. The kids at school wanted candy but there were no candy machines on the campus – only a rule keeping the students from going off campus. Adam had the answer. He invested five dollars in a dozen different kinds of five-cent candies and early one morning at school, but before the class bell rang, he sold them for ten cents apiece. The news that there was candy on campus spread like wildfire and Adam never had need to solicit customers. The venture was a success. In ten or fifteen minutes each morning he recouped his investment and added a five-dollar profit. Everyone was happy: the kids had candy, Adam had an extra five dollars every day, and the grocer who sold him stock every afternoon was happy with the increase in sales. He and Adam became fine friends.

But ventures such as this one involve a certain risk; they are often short-lived and usually end as quickly as they begin. Adam's lasted a month. It ended quite suddenly one morning when one of the hands holding a dime did not particularly want candy, but turned out to be the principal's own. Perhaps it was that he was not satisfied with the flavor of the candy he was given, but whatever the reason, he closed down the business by confiscating what remained of that morning's stock (highway robbery, Adam thought) and by suspending Adam from school for three days.

Although Adam felt the injustice of having his stock confiscated, it was more than made up for by his being suspended. 'What could be more just than this?' he thought, 'To not be allowed to go where I don't want to go in the first place, to have my reputation raised in the eyes of the students by the principal's singular disfavor, and, best of all, to be given three full days to dedicate to my hobby.'

Adam had a rather peculiar hobby. He collected money. But when one speaks politely he says, 'collected coins', or when he speaks with sophistication he says, 'was a numismatist'. Still, it all boiled down to the simple peculiarity that Adam collected money. He was not a miser but he was awfully frugal, and whatever he could, he put into his collection, both in terms of energy and resources. He went through specific and distinct stages in the maturation of his interest and the understanding of its meaning until finally he grew full circle and left his hobby behind him.

His introduction to coin collecting came when, one day in Massachusetts, he discovered a 1919 Lincoln penny in his pocket and began to reflect on all the things that had occurred in that year. He had always loved history and its implications and he knew a fair little bit for a boy his age. 1919 was an interesting year. After getting down a volume of the *Encyclopaedia Britannica* to check something he had forgotten and discover something he had never known, he took his penny to a neighbor whom he knew collected coins. This neighbor was a very genial old man who enjoyed talking with little boys who had more questions than they knew what to do with. Adam liked him and visited him often. But the old man, after questioning Adam all about the year 1919 – which questions he answered proudly – refused to accept the penny. Instead he went into his back room and reappeared with a small blue book. He handed it to Adam and Adam opened it. It was a snap-in book with places for each Lincoln Cent from 1909 to 1979. Each place where the pennies snapped in was labeled with a date and a letter such as 'S' or 'D' (which Adam learned signified where the coin was minted; in this case San Francisco and Denver). There were already a few pennies in place: a 1909, a 1927–D, a 1943–S, and one or two others. The old man had Adam put his penny into the book.

Adam accepted this gift with excitement and enthusiasm; it was a new adventure into history. He did not get home until nightfall and was late for dinner, but at dinner he told all about the gift, and as soon as the meal was finished and the dishes washed, he had everyone empty their pockets onto the table. For each new addition to his collection Adam paid a penny out of his own pocket.

It wasn't long, however, before checking pocket change became insufficient; Adam needed a wider pond to fish from. He took five dollars which he had saved and walked to town one Saturday morning; the bank was open, and there he purchased ten rolls of pennies. He now had five hundred pennies to search through. This proved a much more fruitful field because he began to find older coins also. He continued to buy pennies at the bank and then exchange them again for others; soon he was buying nickel rolls, dime rolls and rolls of quarters too. It was becoming an expensive hobby but it was worth every expense to see another of the slots in one of his little blue books filled.

When Adam's father returned from his tour of duty in Europe he brought with him a sackful of coins – all new and strange – for which Adam had to devise his own means of keeping, cataloguing and displaying. He undertook the challenge and soon began seeking further opportunities to expand this collection. His first goal was to have at least one coin from every country in the world.

Each of Adam's collections afforded him ample opportunity to reflect and ponder. As his collection of foreign coins grew he learned of numerous kings and rulers and wondered if they were just to their people; he looked for their names in the newspapers. He saw many different scripts and tried to learn how to pronounce the few words on each coin; he deciphered those words' meanings. He learned to recognize, understand and translate the different numbering systems such as Arabic and Hebrew. He studied and learned a variety of things implied in the coins: the basic facts and arguments of Islam, for example, or when and why countries changed their names and how revolutions began and ended. The world, as reflected through its coins, called out for Adam to understand it.

There were two aspects of his collection that he always came back to. One was the beauty and history of these pieces of metal that passed through other people's hands unrecognized and unappreciated. The other was that, right up to the moment that a coin became a part of his collection, it had been a part of someone's livelihood or investment, and that although he himself invested his livelihood in these coins they were neither his livelihood nor his investment. They were his vehicle to a wider world than that in which most people were confined.

Visiting his father's friends one summer, Adam discovered that one of them had a Canadian gold piece which he was willing to sell. Adam could and did arrange the money, but the problem was one of getting the coin back into the United States; to do so was illegal at the time. However, it was arranged and done. A few years after Adam's first and only adventure in smuggling the laws were altered and the once restricted foreign gold flowed into the hands of private individuals. The prices trebled overnight on some pieces, but Adam was little inclined to sell the gold he had. He had not bought it to make a profit; he had bought it because he was a collector and that implied a completely different way of looking at money.

His collection continued to grow: although he was always working, he never bought those things that his peers valued. He did not have a car although he could have afforded and used one, he did not even have a bicycle. He had his collections and he had his austerity. He walked or hitch-hiked to work and on his adventures. By the time Adam was eighteen (and kicked out of his parents' house for sleeping in the middle of the day on a mattress that his mother was determined to throw away) his collections were easily worth a few thousand dollars and were safely locked away in a safety deposit box of a bank. When Adam left his parents' house that day he took with him only a few clothes, a few books, and the key to the safety deposit box. But this was the beginning of the end of Adam's peculiar hobby.

He was suddenly face-to-face with the problem of room and board; since he had only recently returned from a short trip to Mexico he had no job and no income to depend upon. His only choice was to sell a piece or two from his collection – it was suddenly his only means of survival. Selling the coins was no problem because they were highly valued, but when people began to try to make a profit out of what were essentially art objects and things of learning, Adam was sorely disappointed. He was not cheated in the prices he received, but other collectors were lowered appreciably in his estimation. Finally he became so exasperated that he exchanged his entire collection with his father – who had always enjoyed the thought of it – for a plane ticket. He went to France to work as a goatherd.

2

In America sex had become one of those subjects both unnatural and uncomfortable to speak about. When sex walks in one door the reasonable spirit walks out the other. For a very long time we engaged in the practice whenever opportunity permitted and we guiltily kept our mouths shut. Then, as wit and drawing-rooms became more common, subtle allusions to sex became frequent drawing-room phenomena at which men were expected to snicker unchastely and women to blush most chastely. Economics. Finally, as progress began to take its daily toll on each and every person, the veils were rent asunder and reference to sex became brazen and explicit. Sex itself became the cause and cure of every problem. We never could find a place for sex in society. We are a pitiful people in this respect.

But this problem is not America's alone. America inherited it from European Christendom, and on the whole struggles with it somewhat more successfully than Europe does. Our religion declared unto its dying day that knowledge was the curse of man (and although this may not be wrong it is generally misunderstood) and that the animal sin of sex passed the curse on from generation to generation. Alas that we should so degrade our religion by mis-understanding both its subtle wisdom and its common sense!

No sooner than the people were beginning to choke on the dust raised by all these foolish feet trampling religion's beauty into the dirt, Freud came, like water under pressure, to clear the air and wash away our misconceptions. Sex was suddenly in vogue. It was – obviously, Freud said – the chief force and most powerful influence in every individual life and the main tension in every society. He only helped us to sink into a mire up to our waists! We could barely move for the mud that clung to us and sucked at us on every side. What choice had we then but to begin to revel in that mud? Adam was chided and ridiculed into the mud by his peers; he was not at all prepared for the experience. His upbringing was, in fact, good. He was actually much better prepared to crawl out than to stay in, except for a stubborn streak in him that refused to allow him to quit any activity until he himself was satisfied that he could succeed in it.

His mother was a religious woman and raised her children to have and keep high morals. She was frank with them about sex but never mentioned passion. She spoke to them openly, clearly, and completely about the matter as though it were any other. But there lay the fundamental falsehood. Because of the great, but hidden, emphasis which everyone put on sex, Adam soon realized that it was not a matter like every other at all. Somewhat secretly it was snickered about at dinner parties and guests were warned that 'little pitchers have big ears'. But Adam understood. The kids talked about it at school behind the buildings and in the bathrooms. There were always rumors and stories and suggestions which no one could really believe but which everyone did. And there was Adam's own body, coupled with a curious mind, that began to have certain desires of its own.

Certainly his mother tried to keep sex in clearly proper bounds, but her very attempt, in a world that had labeled it the be-all and end-all, was in itself a perversity. She tried; you had to give her credit and call her courageous for that. Adam's father, whether wisely or not, never entered the situation at any time. The education of the children was a mother's responsibility. If Adam ever had the audacity to ask his father about these things, he was bluntly referred right back to his mother again.

Adam's journey toward an understanding of sex was one of peril, like a ship passing through dangerous and unknown straits. The seas were ever too shallow and the storm winds ever howling about the sailor's ears and pushing him toward jutting rocks and hidden jaws where he might well be crushed and swallowed. But finally, through the suppression of fear and a smiling fortune, Adam cleared those straits and found himself on a placid and fine sea on their far side. As he looked from horizon to horizon, however, only the barest few sails could be seen of the fleet that had begun the journey with him.

During the Victorian Age it was still possible that a man or a woman might reach the age of legal responsibility chaste and pure. That innocence was the result of cultivated ignorance – the ignorance that a child is born with. In today's society, which has both inherited and rejected Victorian principles, this is no longer possible. Today's loud proclamation of open, free and unrestrained relationships will not tolerate innocence or ignorance in such matters.

Today a child will be pure and chaste through innocence, ignorance and weakness, but an adult cannot be. If a person chooses chastity and purity, it must be a purity brought about through awareness and knowledge, and a chastity that has overcome the unchaste within himself – a chastity, the result of strength and not of weakness. This is the reason why so few choose to walk this difficult road. Adam did finally choose chastity; the cloak he assumed was woven of strength and pain. But this was not for years to come.

He was aware of the sexual tension that roared or purred about him before he actually faced it. He had other pursuits to occupy him and so tried to ignore the noise and tumult as best a young boy is able. He did not allow himself to become enraptured by the crashing melody partly because of his apprehension that he would have to engage himself too closely with other people – a thing which he was always loathe to do – and partly because of his understanding that if he did

engage himself he would have to do so completely. He knew the
tension was not a song that wove in and out of society, but that instead,
it was an all-pervasive buzz that gripped society in its sound.

Adam's collapse of independent will occurred in the classical
way: he succumbed to peer pressure. But let it be said that this one
weakness was so devastating to his spirit that the pain and the hurt
rendered him strong enough to never again relinquish his independence before mere mob opinion. Adam was called a coward and he
listened, once. How many boys have died in wars? how many
crimes have been committed because boys had not the strength of
men to walk the 'coward's gauntlet' unmoved by the sounds of
weak tongues?

He could no longer ignore the buzz that roared. But neither
would he let it penetrate his mind quickly and without a fight. When
he was finally forced to consider girls in a more than playful manner
he was sent into a four-month-long depression. He knew that this
game threatened the very freedom of his seeing. He would pace the
streets late at night with his hands clasped behind his back, his head
bent toward the road. His mind raced and plodded through the
mists of depression; he really had no desire to get involved in this
but he had no choice either. Finally he forced himself to a decision:
he would enter the straits and plunge through them with all the
power and determination he could wield.

He began to find his way to school dances and friends' parties. He
went reluctantly and with trembling in his heart, but also with a
strong will to succeed at the game. He danced because dancing was
the object and he kissed his partners because that was the point. He
knew all the fears and apprehensions, all the little joys and victories,
and all the hopes and petty ambitions that were the rules of play. It
was a terrible time.

Sex was the password to respect. No one could be allowed to
admit to being a virgin. The label was a laughingstock and no one
had the courage to claim it as his own. There was once a day when
young people feared to be labeled anything but a virgin; today fear
reigns among them because one might call another by that
distasteful title and it might stick like feathers thrown on tar. Nor
was sex so very difficult to find in this fear-ridden environment.
Anything a person turns his mind to, he will grow to understand, at
least in some measure; anything that he seeks, he comes to find, at
least in some measure.

*'Because boys had not the strength of men to walk
the coward's gauntlet'*

(William Blake, 'The Blasphemer'; the Tate Gallery, London)

That sex was demanded and required meant that it must be known and not quiet. Stories must be told. False stories would be uncovered by the listeners for any number of reasons: perhaps there were unrealistic or inappropriate details, or perhaps the storyteller – who did not want to be one – had no confidence. But, for whatever reason, the facts were made known even if the truth was not.

Adam sought what he had to and found what he must. He became entrapped by the passions and excitements that entrapped them all. He was entrapped as he knew he would be but a few years before; but now he didn't care. He craved and didn't care.

Adam, a bird who sought the skies, became a rat in a maze. The rat, in seeking its freedom from the puzzle, does not take the shortest or the straightest path. The rat takes every path until it stumbles upon its goal. Like Majnun who sought Layli in the desert sands, Adam sought the beauties of love in the cravings of sex. He only went from madness to madness.

In America double standards abound and truth and fairness are seldom applied. Every woman is taught to be pure and yet how to entice men; every man is told to be 'experienced' but to marry a virgin. Needless to say these expectations do not harmonize well; but much worse than the confusion which they produce for both sexes is the very real fear which they cause among adolescents (who are most prone to fear). Every social situation takes on sexual implications which they will most likely handle incorrectly. Is it any wonder that they are weak and frightened children who jump at shadows and seek psychiatrist's couches when they reach the age of legal maturity?

The few lights on Adam's dark byway were those rare ladies who did not encourage mere sexuality. The first was a girl who opened the gates of his heart with her beauty and pure-heartedness. She appeared in the tunnel of his craving just months before he was compelled to travel to California with his family. But in that short time she drew out from him the first taste of the love that he had bottled up many years before. She was the first of his peers to whom he accorded the respect, love and loyalty due an equal. But their time together was too short for her to become anything more than a passing light on a stormy sea. Adam was fated to sail other passages.

He traveled across the country and began another life. He grew lonely and disconsolate. As the darkness thickened around him once again his passions rose. He had no one to tie him to the mast when stirring songs were sung. He followed the songs into deeper waters. There were intrigues and lies, nightlife and nights when he could have been in his own bed but wasn't. But for all this he was not satisfied. He grew weary of women because he never really knew them. He began to feel the weight of games and charades and untruths; he badly wanted out of the maze but only seemed to get in more deeply. Passion gripped him like a vise which at his every twist and turn grew tighter. He did not grow weary of women's bodies but of women's minds.

When he looked into women's hearts for the strength he could not summon from within his own, he found no courage there, only encouragement. He found it easy to blame them for what was mutual weakness. He never forced a woman into a situation, though his passions often led her; he always asked and did not dispute any answer. Adam was kind.

It was finally this odd kindliness in brutal situations, coupled with a strong dissatisfaction, that led him clear of the dark tunnels of the maze. It happened that a lady whom Adam had grown close to had some reserve of strength which she could summon at the most incongruous moments. This light was dim, like the light of Adam's kindness, but when fused to the friendship that was kindled between them, it grew bright and strong. It shed its strength upon them both. Their friendship was strong because she too was a seeker in an ocean of drifting souls. The paths that she traveled were different from those he sought, but what are different paths to kindred spirits?

With this relationship Adam's sexual energies were channeled and brought more or less under control. He was as satisfied as any man might hope to be when once his *logos* (knowledge) was brought into a reasonable harmony with women's *eros* (relatedness). The stage was set for the moment when he would actively pursue his urge to achieve chastity.

Chastity and purity are not attributes easily gained, but they can be sought. It would yet be years before Adam could call himself chaste (even in the limited sense of the word), but his efforts and strength of decision enabled him to pass beyond the siren's voice and the straits of craving, and come to the sea. The maze dissolved about him and he arose from out the mire – if he was not clean, he was not stuck either – and was on the lighted high road again.

With a little imagination you might be able to accept that Adam was able to throw these two greeds – for gold and for women – from off his back at an early age because of his idealism, his tenacity and his good fortune. But still it would prove difficult to show his casting off the greed for power in the same manner; if, for no other reason, than that power is seldom even revealed to people before their middle years. Indeed, it would be too difficult, and I will not attempt it. I do not need to.

Adam learned as a young child on the playgrounds of the schools that he could be a leader in games if he chose. It was easy because most children would rather follow than tempt the risk of not being followed. Adam chose games from time to time: like the time he designed and arranged the game of 'Blackbeard the Pirate' after the doctor had ordered him to wear an eyepatch over one eye to correct his vision. But usually he did not play the games the other children played because they seldom held his interest for long.

He remembers a conversation he had with himself one day as he was walking home from school. There were a few of his classmates walking and laughing just ahead of him, but he felt no yearning to join in with them. He watched their backs and bobbing heads and told himself, 'It's true: I could be a leader if I wanted to. Once I even wanted to be Pope! But not now. After all, what good is leading a game when as soon as it's over you are no longer the leader? What good is being Pope when the game is over?' He had no ambition to lead in games that ended.

Adam decided after that conversation that leadership and power were not things that he craved. Perhaps his unique heritage gave him both the ability of the ambitious and the ability to ignore ambition. He had no living hero who pulled him towards the alluring scent of power; his only heroes lived in the pages of the history book – those few who still exerted an influence after their deaths. If there were ever to be any power that he would seek it would be that power.

Fame is only the logical extension of power. It is power beyond the limitations of the grave; and it is tempting. But how did a person acquire fame except through power's blunt, coarse ways? Almost everyone who was famous was active in war or politics or something. Was it possible to live a quiet life in a cottage in the hills and still command an influence over other people's lives? There were a few men who had done it: a few inventors and scientists, or a rare philosopher or writer. It was a kind of fame without a name attached, or, if there was a name, it meant something other than the man himself, as in Einstein's Theory or the Socratic Method.

He thought about these conflicting and rather jumbled ideas for a number of years, never quite sure where he stood in relation to them. Did he want fame, did he want solitude, or did he want to reject fame? Some years later while he was in Africa he wrote a short essay on immortality. He has given it to me and I include it here:

ON IMMORTALITY

There was a time when I wanted to be the first person in all the world to think of a thing: something original, something immortal. But I despaired when I realized that by its very nature such a thing is rarer than rare. However, one day, a number of years ago, I was walking along the sidewalk of Thirteenth Street and Griffin Avenue, in a small city in central California, when my shoelace came untied. As I bent down to retie it there came to me something new, something unique, something that would give me immortality among men, something . . . about shoelaces!

But as I stood up again it was gone; gone as quickly as it had come. I was crushed. I could not remember what it was, and to this day I still can't recall. Immortality is such a fleeting thing.

CHAPTER VI

*Being how Adam, heretofore a loner, cultivates
friendship*

And it came to pass after these things, that the butler of the king of
Egypt and his baker had offended their lord the king of Egypt. And
Pharaoh was wroth against two of his officers, against the chief of
the butlers, and against the chief of the bakers. And he put them in
ward in the house of the captain of the guard, into the prison, the
place where Joseph was . . .

And they dreamed a dream both of them, each man his dream in
one night . . . the butler and the baker of the king of Egypt, which
were bound in the prison. And Joseph came in unto them in the
morning, and looked upon them, and behold, they were sad. And
he asked Pharaoh's officers that were with him in the ward of his
lord's house, saying, Wherefore look ye so sadly today? And they
said unto him, We have dreamed a dream, and there is no
interpreter of it. And Joseph said unto them, Do not interpretations
belong to God? tell me them, I pray you . . .

And it came to pass the third day, which was Pharaoh's birthday,
that he made a feast unto all his servants: and he lifted up the head of
the chief butler and the chief baker among his servants. And he
restored the chief butler unto his butlership again; and he gave the
cup into the Pharaoh's hand: But he hanged the chief baker: as
Joseph had interpreted to them. Yet did not the chief butler
remember Joseph but forgat him.

Genesis 40: 1–8, 20–23

I

For sixteen years Adam had been alone. He lived alone in his world
of reflections; he traveled alone beside his family; alone he dreamed
his dreams; and alone he spoke with the clouds and to the night.
Aloneness had become a part of his soul – he was all-in-one.

Although he did not know it yet, no matter how close he might come to another human being, no matter how fine their relationship might grow, still, in the deepest part of himself he would be alone. He would no longer be alone because of reserve and wariness, but because of nature herself. She has decreed that the body will house the soul but that it will neither hold it nor fully express it; it is ultimately inexpressible and walks alone in a limbo unto its God.

For sixteen years Adam had also been lonely. He wanted to share who he was with another human being; he wanted to know the inside of another intimately; he wanted to see if they were the same. But for sixteen years he had not found another person who also wanted this. There were some few who were kind or sympathetic. But this was not enough for him; he wanted all, and he would not settle for any portion less than all.

One day in Eureka Adam walked into a new class and discovered Richard. Richard was blonde and lanky and did not fit. But what really piqued Adam's interest was a conversation which he had the opportunity to overhear where Richard was trying to explain in his cocksure way the relationship between the spirit of a Jaguar (the automobile) and the actual nuts and bolts that it was made of. Adam was intrigued because, although he knew nothing about cars in general or Jaguars in particular, he did know something about spirit and, apparently, so did Richard.

Adam made a point of joining the conversation and it continued throughout the class hour; it being a quiet conversation in one corner, the teacher droned on without taking appreciable notice or offense. Perhaps somewhere in the back of her mind she understood that it was much more important than the ridiculous lecture she was delivering about toilet seats and venereal disease.

This conversation raised the possibility of a true friendship developing between Adam and Richard. Richard's friend, Chip, didn't really figure in the discussion because he was stoned and more interested in giggling at the lecture on toilet seats. It wasn't too long before he moved closer to the front of the room where he could heckle more audibly. Adam and Richard talked on; by the time the class ended Richard had invited Adam to his house that afternoon to show him the Jaguar which he and Chip were in the process of rebuilding.

As Adam walked beneath the cedar trees near Richard's home he thought about what was going to happen. His mind replayed their conversation and he found that he liked Richard all the more because of it. Richard was obviously a person who didn't come by his opinions easily and whose opinions, when once formed, were not run of the mill. There seemed to be a lot more to him than he showed, and yet which he did not seem to be afraid to show if the right person be found. But the most important of Richard's attributes was his attitude toward his friend, Chip. Adam had not seen much of Chip, but he had seen that love and he liked it.

He had no intention of dislodging Chip from Richard's heart but he did swear to himself that, if Richard turned out to be the kind of person Adam thought he might, then he would do his level best to forge a place in that heart for himself and give his own heart in return. As it turned out, Chip was moving to New Zealand, and Adam and Richard grew to love one another.

Their friendship developed slowly, gradually, nobly. What need was there to rush something that would be because it was destined to be? They each led their own lives: Richard had his cars – after the Jaguar there were others – and Adam had his interests. Richard was a year younger than Adam and so they never again shared the same classes; they seldom even saw each other at school, but then school was an alien ground and not conducive to great developments. Their friendship flowered in the more eternal aspect of the night over a chess board, a cold greasy pizza, and a philosophy that arose out of the day's activities. They each saved the day's great thoughts to share with each other. Winters were spent walking the deserted streets in midnight's mist and drizzle. Springs and autumns passed at two in the morning on the swings of a nearby elementary school.

'Why', Adam thought, 'did it take so long to come to this town? What would it have been like to have been born here, among these friends? These friends!'

For a long time Adam had known that this was an age of enlightenment, an age of possibilities. But at the same time he had been disappointed because he seldom, if ever, met people who believed in those possibilities and that enlightenment. Most lacked the faith and the courage to become who they could be or fully do what they were capable of doing. This generation was a disappointment. Until he came to Eureka. Was this town really different or was it that only now he had the ability to recognize and appreciate other people's initiatives and endeavors?

For the first time in his life he had friends whom he respected and in whom he believed. He felt that each one of them had the potential to do something great for himself and for the world. Each of them radiated creative energy. It was good to be among them.

Richard was the nucleus of the group, but for no reason that anyone could pinpoint; perhaps he was simply the most constant among the core. The core was composed of six people. Richard who would, as likely as not, one day be a philosopher-hero. Rosemary Derryberry who had been in high school for six years and was beginning to tire of it – she could not bring herself to concentrate on things she didn't enjoy – but who had developed a wonderful harmony in her tender-sweet lisp that oozed folksongs and her guitar strings that rippled original individuality. One day confidence and good fortune would come together for Rosie and the world would find itself a little more caring for all her sadness. Chip (while he was still there) usually looked more dead than alive because he was always either stoned or getting stoned or – on official family occasions – trying to recover from being stoned. If Chip survived he would fulfill his part. Kate was an actress of no little talent or beauty or brains but she would probably settle right there in Eureka with Carl or some other steady man. Carl was, if he was anything at all, steady. He was as steady as Adam was transient, as solid as Adam was ethereal. He maintained a 3.89 grade point average. He was small, wiry, and his shirt dripped like ice-cream from a cone; still, there was genius lurking beneath his mop of uncombed hair. He was solid but crazy; Adam was sure that these two attributes were intimately related. If, when Carl became a nuclear physicist, he did not outdo Einstein in sheer perseverance, he would yet outdo him in character antics. The sixth member of the core was Adam himself who had high ambitions, but who could never quite explain where it was he was going. These six were the remnant of last year's drama club, a music class or two and the library's brainstorming, barnstorming, brain drain. This was what America was coming to.

Around these came and went numerous other notorious personities. Most passed in and out through Richard's capable hands. He was no respecter of persons but accepted everyone in some way. If someone struck his fancy he invited him to a party. Those invited stayed until it was time for them to be going on.

The parties, like the group, were mellow. If anyone had money there was wine available; if no one did, there was tea; Rosie always had her guitar and Chip always had his pipe. Adam often nursed a pipe of tobacco and Richard was occasionally delegated to a distant corner because he had brought a cigar along. Kate and Carl all but made love in front of the fire.

Sometimes these parties were a celebration of something important like the day the swallows returned to Capistrano, or the anniversary of President Nixon's resignation; sometimes they were a celebration of something that only seemed important like the school administration's acceptance of a petition for advanced placement classes, or rave reviews in the local newspaper of a play in which one of them was acting; sometimes a party just happened because somebody asked Rosie to play and somebody else made tea and put a log on the fire.

These were Adam's friends and he was honored by them. Theirs was a bond of sad music, weak wine and crackling fires. It was a bond that would never die . . . even when the friends were no more.

Their relationship helped each of them to mature and become strong emotionally, intellectually and spiritually. Richard and Adam had become brothers. But even brothers must come to a parting of ways. They were two skaters on a figure-eight track who came together for a brief moment at the crux of their lives. Their parting happened not once, but a number of times, each time cutting another of the arteries that held their hearts together. And yet, at the end, with the last artery severed, still there was something that could not be severed, something that was as eternal as its creation.

Their first parting was one of love. Adam went to France and on the eve of his leaving he was not with his family, or at a loud party, but with his friend sharing the silence.

Although distance need not end a relationship, still, when people are young and their heads are high they travel fast and far; if they are not together to share their travels, they travel apart. Adam returned from France and visited Eureka for a few weeks before leaving again. He found just how far apart he and Richard had traveled. One Friday evening they sat in Richard's car in an empty downtown alley and watched the people's Friday games. As they sat, they talked. As they talked, they realized their distance and tried to talk about it. But no back-tracking could be done; they each believed too strongly in their own path. The scene was poignant and their distance most dramatically revealed when it came to a discussion of drugs. Although neither Richard nor Adam indulged excessively, still it was a part of their lives. More than a year before Adam had decided to give drugs up completely, and although he made no public declaration of the fact, it was known, and known most especially by Richard. What Richard did not know was how very distasteful Adam had begun to consider their use; being away from alcohol and drugs for a lengthy period had cleared his head of their influence. He had grown strong views about their detrimental effect on individuals and society.

Richard bluntly said that Adam was becoming self-righteous and spoke to him about the glow of a bottle of wine or a few joints shared with a friend in the evening. He knew that this was the kind of argument to which Adam was susceptible; he knew that Adam was an incurable romantic. But Adam hardened his heart to these entreaties and would not consider them realistic. He explained that the little he had indulged was enough for him to see that it did him no good, that it was not a part of his path. Richard, on the other hand, declared that the little he had explored convinced him that there lay something to be found but that it would demand greater involvement. He was determined to take that step. They lapsed into silence as another bond was severed; and Adam remembered a passage from the New Testament which he had heard numerous times as a child: that in 'those days shall the sun be darkened, and the moon shall not give her light, and the stars shall fall from heaven . . . then shall two be in the field; and one shall be taken and the other left'.

Two years later Adam again returned to Eureka for a short while and he and Richard worked together for a month in a cannery. He tried to tell Richard of the religion he had joined and of how widely it had expanded his horizons. But it was no use. Religion had become too difficult a strain on their relationship. Adam left California again early one afternoon, stopping at Richard's house before leaving town, but Richard was asleep after his night's work. Adam left a message which read:

> I am leaving today. I stopped by to see you
> but you were sleeping. Are you still sleeping?

He was never really sure what impish desire impelled him to write those particular words, but he was pretty sure that they had made Richard angry. Later he repented and sent his friend a copy of Toynbee's *History*. In it he inscribed these words from another book:

He is the Strong, the Well-Beloved!
O light of truth, Ḥisám-i-Dín, the bounteous,
No prince hath the world begot like unto thee!

I am wondering why the tie of love was so abruptly severed, and
the firm covenant of friendship broken. Did ever, God forbid, My
devotion lessen, or My deep affection fail, that thou hast thus forgot
Me and blotted Me from thy thoughts?

'What fault of Mine hath made thee cease thy favors?
Is it that We are lowly and thou of high degree?'*

Adam was later asked by his mother why he and Richard never
saw each other when they had once been the closest of friends. He
answered that it was natural that their ways should part because
they had become very different people. When his mother probed
further he said that Richard had become a working-class intellectual
and that he himself had become a mystic. Then he added with mixed
vehemence and sadness, 'We could not agree about Justice.'

Three years later in New Delhi, I met Adam one afternoon in a
restaurant. He was just finishing some writing and there were tears
in his eyes. I asked him if anything was wrong and he handed me this
letter to read:

Richard,
I picked up a copy of Lin Yutang's *The Importance of Living* and
have been reading through the night. It was your father's book as I
recall; and it has brought back wonderful memories of philosophy,
arguments, and smoke. I once told you that I loved you – not mere
words, but words that are spoken infrequently and are not easy to
speak. I might be fool enough to cast away friendship for philosophical reasons; but I cannot cast away love.

Between men and women the parting of first love is crushing and
the winds cry in regret at those moments; such was our parting, for
we had separate paths to follow. But paths can go in circles and lead
us to where we were with wider eyes.

I do not say that I have changed: mellower, more passionate at
times, but probably still self-righteous. I believe what I believe with
all my heart and soul, but my beliefs are always changing. I am a
child. The further words not inscribed in Toynbee were: 'Or is it
that a single arrow hath driven thee from the battle?'

* Bahá'u'lláh, quoting Rúmí and Sa'dí, *The Four Valleys*.

We are both too easily hurt, and we too easily hurt. For all the fortresses and stable mysteries that we erected, Achilles was felled by a single arrow. But, for all that, I still offer my love – it shall always be there.

The Moth

The moth lies
dying;
      its wings fluttering
against the hard wood floor.

A victim of its passion,
    it fills the night
      with a sound like footfall
        and raindrops,

Then only the pregnant silence
      of surrender,
   as the candle flickers on.

Adam.

2

One of the people whom Richard invited to a party was a girl who lived near him. She was a chubby, freckled and smiling potter. She was honest, sincere and happy. When she was light-hearted she was simple and refreshing. When she was heavy-hearted she was quiet and had two big, watery, brown eyes. Her name was Diana and Adam liked her from the moment they met. Although she was shy, like Adam, she did not play games. After the party, when all the others had gone off somewhere, and Adam was talking, obviously with no intention of doing anything else, she took him in her arms and had him down on the floor, covered with sloppy, wet kisses before he knew what had happened.

Slowly they grew to know each other very well, and gradually they came to keep regular company, spending more nights together than apart. They grew to be friends and lovers; they shared their

84

hearts with each other. They appreciated each other's abilities and potentials; they loved each other for their talents and they listened to each other's dreams.

Before Adam met Diana he had begun to tire of women's minds. Secretly he had begun to despise their vanities and their pretended weaknesses. He hated their games and dreaded the day he would meet a female who played the games so subtly that he might not recognize them. More than once he had left some seemingly poor creature, tears flowing down her cheeks to be checked only by an inadequately used (or was it deftly handled) handkerchief, as she sobbed inanities in a corner somewhere. He turned on his heel and walked away in disgust. He delegated such tasks to God – such people either recovered or died, either way it was not his business – let God handle it!

Then he met Diana, and she was honest. Even more important she was sincere. If she cried, she cried alone and asked for no one's help. She solved her own problems. She held that it was each person's right to fight his own battles; and she never delegated that right or shied away from it. Her strength attracted Adam much more than her tears would have.

They talked a great deal. Between Diana and Richard, Adam talked and thought and listened himself into exhaustion; it was good. For the first time in his life Adam began to appreciate the complexity and subtlety of a woman's being. Diana would undoubtedly see a problem or a situation from an angle that he could not; she could explain her view adequately and completely, and could make Adam understand it. Their sexual relationship was an example of this; from their different ways of seeing, they found a level of agreement and chose a solution together. Such exercises soon made him appreciate, not only Diana, but other women as well.

Freed from the grip of his sexual desire for other women and their appeal for him, he came to appreciate women in a wholly new way. Diana gave him back much of what he had lost when he entered the sexual entanglement. And there was more that she would give him yet.

They loved each other, but with a quiet kind of love that didn't grate or repel or drown with its sentiment or lavishness. Their love blossomed while sitting in the shade of an ancient oak and sharing dreams of France, in walking for miles along a rail line and finally resting and eating in the high grass that overgrew a neglected apple orchard.

Their lives were different and their paths led different ways. Both understood this. But their paths ran together for a while and they walked together until the road's fork appeared ahead of them. They were not saddened by this inevitability, instead, they appreciated all the more the hour they were given to grow together. Their love was simple and unconfined.

Both Adam and Diana had been born students of life's mysteries. Diana was an artist and a craftsman; she studied pottery. Adam was a poet and studied religion. When it came time that he choose his religion she supported him, was tender and understood. They were walking down the sidewalk toward his house late one night when he told her, 'I became a Bahá'í last night.'

She was silent for a while and then said, 'That's the last thing I would have expected. You always argued with them so much; and I liked your arguments more than theirs.'

'So did I sometimes. But they were right. I had no choice.' Silence ensued for a few more minutes; then he began again, 'There are some laws that I found out about today. I can't drink any more.'

'That won't be a problem; you hardly drink at all now.'

'No drugs.'

'You gave up smoking six months ago. Is tobacco okay?'

'Yeh.'

'That's good. You like your pipe.'

They walked on. After another block Diana asked, 'I suppose that means no more sex, too?' It was hard to know what kind of intonation she had applied to the question; maybe it really was neutral.

'Only after marriage.'

'Oh.' And she lapsed into thought again. They were both sensitive to each other's needs and wants. It was much better that she had spoken this implication of Adam's decision herself. It would have proven very difficult for him to say it to her.

'Well, it's better if I go home now,' she began, 'I am happy for you. You have found something that you have been searching for for a long time. The way you've chosen is not going to be easy, but you'll make it, I know you will. You're lucky. Maybe I'll find what I'm looking for one day too. Don't walk me home. It's too far and I want some time alone to think. I love you.' And she kissed him. Then she turned and walked away.

CHAPTER VII

*Being how Adam relates to the author the story of
rats at High Mass and of his tumbling down a
stairway*

Then Pharaoh sent and called Joseph, and they brought him hastily
out of the dungeon; and he shaved himself, and changed his
raiment, and came in unto Pharaoh. And Pharaoh said unto Joseph,
I have dreamed a dream, and there is none that can interpret it: and I
have heard say of thee, that thou canst understand a dream to
interpret it. And Joseph answered Pharaoh, saying, It is not in me:
God shall give Pharaoh an answer of peace . . .

And the thing was good in the eyes of Pharaoh, and in the eyes of
all his servants. And Pharaoh said unto his servants, Can we find
such a one as this is, a man in whom the Spirit of God is? And
Pharaoh said unto Joseph, Forasmuch as God hath shewed thee all
this, there is none so discreet and wise as thou art: Thou shalt be
over my house, and according unto thy word shall all my people be
ruled: only in the throne will I be greater than thou. And Pharaoh
said unto Joseph, See, I have set thee over all the land of Egypt. And
Pharaoh took off his ring from his hand, and put it upon Joseph's
hand, and arrayed him in vestures of fine linen, and put a gold chain
about his neck; And he made him to ride in the second chariot
which he had; and they cried before him, Bow the knee: and he
made him ruler over all the land of Egypt.

Genesis 41:14–16, 37–43

I

Even the most superficial study of history will suffice to prove that
religion has always been the most powerful and influential force in
the progress and development of humanity and of individuals.
Sometimes it has been creative and sometimes destructive, but
always the most powerful force. Only the blindest and most

stubborn of observers will not acknowledge its precedence in power to shape and to change.

Man's greatest endeavors and accomplishments are a direct reflection of his search after the unknowable. He has ever had an element of dissatisfaction within him. He seeks contentment by reaching for what he cannot grasp. If a person is sated he grows nervous and feels out of place, for his place is to be ever emptying himself that he may be refilled. He is a sparkling fountain in a green gardenland that must ever throw its life-giving waters high into the air in order to be refilled again from the hidden spring. He is a hollow reed and must be an instrument of ever-flowing movement or, like the reed, he will grow hard and brittle. If he does not throw himself beyond himself he cracks and breaks and dies. Man denies his nature if he does not reach beyond his own understanding; if he does not, he is less than a man.

A person is judged by the cause he promotes; a cause is judged by whether or not it is greater than the one who promotes it. Further, all men are searching for the cause in which they might sacrifice themselves, but only a few find it. Historically, religion has always been such a cause. It has offered man the opportunity to rise and reach beyond himself, and to sacrifice himself totally to the reaching. Religion is man's attempt to search after the greatest unknown of all: God. God is the ultimate unknowable Essence. God has never been known by man and never will be. Every mystic, every seer, every saint has strayed far from the path of the knowledge of God. And it will ever be so.

What, then, is the greater challenge, the greater cause, the greater sacrifice than this? Its very impossibility defines it; its very impossibility draws man to sacrifice himself before its ungainable goal. It fulfills his deepest nature. The great attraction of the search after an unknowable God is what gives religion its power and its force. Its fulfillment of man's greatest need gives it precedence over all the forces that shape and change man and men.

2

Though apostates are not good judges of their former religion, they have a story to tell. Adam's mother was a Roman Catholic. Her children were brought up as Catholics. They attended the Mass regularly, they went to catechism, they played and participated in the parish events. But at the end of it all, when they reached the age of discretion, they turned away from the Church. Children turn their noses at odors that propriety refuses to let adults acknowledge.

When Adam was seven years old he was an ardent believer. He kneeled and stood and sat, he sang the songs loudly, and received communion every week. He spent many hours trying to think up sins to confess on Saturday evening in preparation for Mass on Sunday morning. It was difficult to think up good sins because he was only a child and didn't have much chance to sin.

One week he decided that he was going to learn the Lord's Prayer. This was the first important religious experience in his life. He told me about it one cold, winter evening in New Delhi, India. He said:

'I was seven years old and in my second year at a Catholic primary school. I possessed a child's ignorance and a child's devotion. The event which first challenged my ignorance and my devotion occurred at Mass one Sunday morning in late spring.

'I remember listening to the high, excited chirping of the sparrows as we walked across the yard to the church; I remember the unpredictable, swooping flight of the swallows; and I remember wondering if long, long ago the first robin had been cut by a knife or an arrow and if that had caused all the robins to have blooded breasts.

'I had spent the entire week preparing for this day. I had memorized the Lord's Prayer; more than that, I had understood it. The joy of understanding and the pride of accomplishment made me excited, nervous and unusually sensitive to the environment and events around me.

'The Mass began and flowed in its ancient rhythm, sometimes dull, sometimes pitched, but ever growing in tempo toward its climax. The priest said, "Let us pray."

'We began in unison, "Our Father, Who art in Heaven, hallowed be Thy Name . . ." but soon all awareness of the voice of the congregation faded and I heard only my own. It was strong and clear – no longer the mere murmer of nonsensical syllables that it had always been before. It bore witness to understanding.

'As the prayer left our lips and disappeared, resounding off the ornamental stone, the stained oak and the stained glass, my heart heaved a sigh of completeness. I looked up at my mother, wanting to share the understanding, but found only a mother's loving smile – her eyes were quiet and no spark of the Undeniable burned in them.

She had said the prayer but she had not understood it. My heart, in the midst of its rejoicing, clutched and tore at itself; the earth trembled at my feet.

'I turned and gazed at the others in the congregation but found only dulled eyes and bored masks. They too, I realized, had only said the prayer, repeated the ritual; they had not understood it. With that first realization, through rapidly misting eyes, I saw the earth gape at my feet. It divided as if a great cleaver had descended splitting it asunder. An ever-widening chasm formed and in helpless despair I watched as my mother, my sister, and all the congregation drifted away from me. They noticed nothing. They heedlessly sang their Job's praises unto the Lord that set them adrift, marooned.

'It would be years before I realized that it was I who had been set adrift, I who was alone on an island, I who would have to find a way back.'

Now, although he followed the same devotions as before – Mass, catechism, the other activities – his eyes were wary and his heart questioning. Nothing was any longer accepted just because it was. His questions could not be answered – the priests, and the nuns and the teachers could not be blamed for that – they were ultimately unanswerable. But Adam did blame them for insisting that their incomplete answers were right and whole. Their little was enough for them, and if they could, they would have it be enough for him also. He blamed them for being satisfied.

'Who wrote the Gospels?'

'God wrote them.'

'But men wrote them. How could God write them?'

'God filled the men with the Holy Spirit and wrote the Gospels through them.'

'My school-teacher said that man created God, not God created man?'

'Your teacher was confused!'

'I guess I'm confused too.'

'You shouldn't be. God wrote the Gospels. You should listen to me.'

Or:

'I heard that there were other Gospels that the Church didn't accept?'

'There are only four Gospels that you should concern yourself with.'

Or:

'How could Jesus rise from the dead? It doesn't make any sense?'

'Jesus was God. He could do anything.'

'It still doesn't make any sense.'

'You should pray about it.'

Or a hundred other questions with no answers. Adam was best liked at the church when he kept his mouth shut and his questions to himself. They confused the other children, he was told. Many years later Adam was shown a copy of the Catechism on a Nile steamer by a Sudanese grammar school student who asked about the meaning of an English word. Adam borrowed the little book for the day and read it through. He thought it was a wonderful, mystical treatise on the station of Christ and His relationship to God and His Church, and the Church's relationship to Him. Each sacrament was a symbol of man's reaching toward God.

The problem is that it was taught and not learned. A thing as mystical as the dogma and doctrine of the Catholic Church cannot be taught to children and laymen. When it is, then its symbols become frozen facts. It becomes a clay vessel without the water that keeps it young: it becomes hard and brittle; soon cracks begin to appear. Each word becomes dry of the spirit which it should carry. The letter of the Word kills; the spirit conveys life. It would be much better if the children were taught to think and ponder for themselves, to see and make analogies; to listen to others but to accept nothing as clear and granted simply because other people have expressed it so. Each child should be taught to freely investigate with both his heart and his mind and only when the two agree on something should he accept it. Even when he accepts it, he should be taught to accept it as relative, and open to modification as his understanding widens. Each child should be taught that each word has a hundred different meanings.

If only this were done then a day would come when the child would discover the catechism for himself. Then it would be a very different thing for him. If this were done then the Catholic Church would again be more alive than dead.

In the Spring Adam and I met again, as we had arranged, at the Ajanta Caves not too far from Aurangabad. Here, we three (my son was with us), as part of a tour, visited the ancient Buddhist chambers and temples. But when our tour bus readied to leave we decided to stay on. The spirit that created Ajanta is lost to the millions who visit there each year; they are tourists visiting a popular historical site. But to walk that horseshoe canyon beyond the last rock-hewn chamber, beyond even where the occasional tourist takes his daily constitutional, is to find, amidst boulders seemingly hurled there by God to stand witness to the passing ages and centuries, a spring-green pool half cast in shadow by the looming cliffs, half in light, gently coaxing the wanderer to touch its serene and ancient depths while the waterfall that created it begins to eclipse the noise and tumult between those first monks and today's wanderer.

Adam and I wandered away from our tour and approached the pool in the early afternoon. We sat down in the shade and mist. As we listened to the quiet roar and splatter of the falls and watched the silent pool welcome and absorb the rushing, excited gift of the falls, our thoughts and words turned to the monks who found this canyon and spent their lives carving into its soft stone walls their dedication to the Buddha. Theirs was an inspiring example of worship and search.

Slowly our minds returned to our lives and we spoke to each other of our religious experiences and growth. Surely there could have been no more appropriate place in all the world to gather together, reflect on, and tell our stories. There was, for me, a definite impression of *déjà vu* about the place and the experience. When Adam told me of his adventures it was as if I had heard them before. These were the stories he told as we sat beneath the waterfall:

He said, 'I have often been asked, particularly by Persian Bahá'ís, to tell how I became a Bahá'í. Because they are, more often than not, born into Bahá'í families they think they have missed the opportunity to search and find the Cause through their efforts. I often find myself telling them that recognizing the station of Bahá'u'lláh is not the end and conclusion of the great yearning. It is only the first step. They must learn to appreciate and be confident in their own growth; we are all searching to draw nearer.

'I only wish I knew how to say that the most important thing is to keep our religion young, fresh and green within them, let its power and influence spring from their undiminished yearning after understanding and service; that if we don't do this our Faith will become like a dried flower and we will become the fanatical faithful who stone the Prophets and point out heresy. I wish I could help each one of them to arise with a revolutionary's fervor to change the

'A spring-green pool half cast in shadow by the looming cliffs,
half in light, gently coaxing the wanderer to touch its serene
and ancient depths'

(Figure of Kuan-yin, Sung dynasty; The Ashmolean Museum, Oxford)

world; then they wouldn't feel they were missing anything. Perhaps the most efficient way to do this is to realize and admit that we, as Bahá'ís, do not have a monopoly on Truth; and to learn to accept other religions and spiritual philosophies with joy and devotion. This is what Bahá'u'lláh taught.

'At any rate, I have told this story numberless times, but seldom fully and completely. Sometimes time has limited the telling, sometimes interests have redirected it or led me to concentrate on one part and eliminate another. But today everything is combined to help me tell all.

'I think I told you some time ago of the episode of the Lord's Prayer and its consequences for me. After that, my heart wept for the remaining seven years that I still considered myself a Catholic. My questions were not answered and were often ignored entirely. Slowly, as the years wore on, the spirit of rebellion grew stronger in me. After my eleventh or twelfth year I continued to attend the Mass but only at my mother's insistence. I seldom took the communion. As a young child the meagerness of the sacrament (as food) frustrated me; during these years the symbolism repelled me. The dwelling on blood and body made the wafer and the wine distasteful. It seemed as if the Church carried primitive pagan superstition into the modern ritual. I was ashamed of its unenlightened attitude.

'Although I still attended the Mass, I was permitted, as a concession, to sit in the back of the church rather than the front where my mother and sister habitually sat. From there I could watch more and participate less. Then something happened on the Christmas following my fourteenth birthday that proved to be my release from having to attend a service I was no longer interested in. It happened at a midnight Mass and a High Mass. It was a very special occasion, one of the two most important Masses of the year. But I was feeling rather put out by it all because I did not sit for long that night in my usual spot in the rear pew. I thought that with all the pageantry and excitement I wouldn't be missed. I wasn't missed; I was found.

'I was audacious that night; I had smuggled a book in with me. My choice of reading material at that time was not of a high caliber: the name of the book I was engrossed in was *Willard*. It was a popular story (soon to be made into a movie) about a deranged and lonely man who befriends and trains a pack of rats to aid him in his nefarious designs of revenge. It was probably the very horribleness

of the story that attracted me. But whatever reason I had for reading
that book proved stronger than any reason I could think of to stay at
the Mass. I went to a lounge at the back of the church and began to
read there. As if it were not unsettling enough that I left a Christmas
High Mass to read a disgusting novel about rats, I lay down on one
of the couches in the lounge to read comfortably too! Of course, the
only reasonable thing to do when you are alone on a couch is to lie
down; but some people believe that couches were only made for
sitting – to lie down on a couch is tantamount to heresy.

'Not long after I had comfortably arranged myself and was once
again engrossed in that fascinating story, I was suddenly jolted from
its perverse unreality to an even more perverse reality. One of the
parish priests entered the room and saw me lying down. He
bellowed at the sight. Apparently I did not rise to his authority quite
fast enough because he charged like a bull. I was no more than
halfway into a sitting position when I was suddenly grabbed by the
front of my shirt (I lost a button to the experience), hauled through
the air and half thrown to my feet. I was quite awake by then,
although still mystified about what was happening. At the risk of
sounding cliché'd I have to describe the man as a brawny giant – I
only came up to his chest – with a thick Irish accent. He was a bully.
He was not at all my idea of a priest but he was wearing the correct
garments so I wisely refrained from challenging his authority to
manhandle me. He apparently thought it was within his rights. My
wisdom and restraint certainly did nothing to appease him. He was
determined to be angry. "What are you doing here?"
'"Reading," I replied.
'"What are you doing lying down?"
'"Reading," I repeated, thinking that he must be having as much
trouble understanding my English as I had understanding his.
'"I always thought you were a smart ass!"
'There was nothing much I could say to that. Even if I had said
something, he probably would not have been in the mood to
appreciate it.
'"Are you supposed to be at Mass?" His tone was becoming even
more aggressive.
'"Yes."
'"Then why aren't you there?"
'I knew he wouldn't understand but I had to tell him anyway, "I
felt like reading."

'He let loose of my collar with one hand – the other was still strong enough to hold me dangling like a puppet on a string just above the floor – and pressed the freed index finger under my nose. "I feel like punching you in the nose!"

'There wasn't much I could say to that either. I was beginning to feel like the ninety-eight pound weakling who has just had sand kicked in his face: beginning to seethe with anger but still absolutely unable to express it. "Let go of me!" I demanded. He took no notice.

'"What is that book?" he said releasing the strangle-hold and grabbing my book. As he looked at the cover he realized that he actually did have a case against me. With a sadistic half-snarl, half-smile he ordered, "Get out of the church! Go to your car."

'"What about my book?"

'"I'll give it to your mother. Now get out!" and he hauled me to the door of the church.

'For the better part of an hour I anxiously waited for Mass to finish. I had to sit beside the car because the doors were locked. Although my mother was a good Catholic she must have believed in the Hadith of the Prophet Muhammad: Trust in God but tie your camel; that car was never left unlocked, even in the church parking lot. But even if I had been able to sit in the car with the light on and even if I had had my book, still I would not have been able to read. My mind was racing with anger, nervous expectation and just plain excitement.

'Finally the Mass was over and all the parishioners came trooping out. A few looked questioningly at me as they walked by. My mother and sister did not appear. Soon all the other cars had left the parking lot. My mother finally emerged from the church carrying my book. She did not look particularly happy. I wondered if she would remember that this was Christmas Eve.

'She reached the car and unlocked the doors without speaking. My sister gave me a look that said: "Oh boy! Are you in trouble!" After we got into the car my mother handed me my book saying, "Here's your book. I am ashamed of you!" And that was all. Everyone remained silent during the drive home. My sister was disappointed: she had expected fireworks and got subtlety. My mother never said another thing about that night, but never again forced me to attend the Mass. My sister envied my luck. I was suddenly free from the hold of the Church and that was important to me. I have often wondered just exactly what the priest said to my mother. I don't suppose I'll ever find out.'

He stopped and listened in silence to the waterfall for a few moments before continuing.

'So there I was, an outcast, eyes weary with seven years' tears yet still wet behind the ears. Now there was no more reason to cry. My tears had run to join their strength to a tumultuous ocean; I was cast into the sea from a beleaguered ship; not, however, like Jonah who was thrown into the sea because he told his shipmates that he had tried to escape from his God; I was thrown in because I had told my shipmates that they had tried to escape from their God.

'But it was not long before I brought things into perspective and set myself on the long course toward land. At that time I enjoyed a reputation for being able to rationalize anything and everything. This ability came in very handy: I looked things over really well and decided that the best place to begin was at the beginning, by searching and deciding if there even was a God! I called myself an atheist (for simple honesty's sake) and set about to find a proof of whether God existed at all. I had some support for choosing this particular starting point: my father, as best I could judge, was also an atheist. He had been cajoled into going to church one Christmas many years before, but even that once he had refused to kneel, claiming that he had once injured his leg in an automobile accident and so could not without a good deal of pain.

'Once, and only once, I asked my father if he believed in God. I was seven years old and just learning to play chess; he was driving me to a friend's house to play a few games.

'From out of nowhere I asked him, "Do you believe in God?"

'"Yes." He was probably under orders!

'"Then why don't you go to church?"

'"Because I don't believe in churches. Here's your friend's house."

'But as I thought back on that short conversation – and I thought about it many times – I came to the conclusion that he didn't really believe in God at all. He only said that he did so that I wouldn't worry, and would stop asking questions, and so that he wouldn't have to answer my mother if another response filtered back to her. I was sure my father was an atheist and I was equally sure that when I declared myself an atheist also, he chuckled inside himself. My mother cried.

'Does God exist? It's a mighty big question for a fourteen-year-old to solve. But it became my challenge and I grew to enjoy it. Things must be arranged in an order of importance; when things of this order come up, then things of lesser importance – like classes in school – must be put to one side. But I had no objection to that. At the far end of the school compound was a small stream and a few over-hanging trees. Most people didn't go there so I found it a good place to lie down on my back and wonder about God. In that pleasant retreat school bells were so distant that they could no longer infringe upon my thoughts.

'When I was somewhat younger I had had a teacher who claimed that men had created God rather than the other way around. It was a fascinating claim, and one that I spent a long time pondering. He had also claimed at one point – we were studying China at the time – that the Chinese had developed three major religions: Taoism, Confucianism, and Buddhism; further, that the three were the ideal emanation of the Chinese mind, because the doctrines of the Tao appealed to youth, the doctrines of Confucius appealed to the person of middle years, and that someone preparing for and meditating upon death was most strongly attracted to Buddhism. This was an interesting reflection on the Chinese character and on religion, but the problem was that if man created God and religion out of his own need, then why didn't he do it in a more reasonable manner? Why create three religions and such potential for confusion and conflict? Why not create a single God and one religion that would satisfy a man throughout his life? These things simply did not follow a logical progression – if man had created God, he would have created Him in a more elastic mode. I still had not understood God or men!

'Gradually my thoughts were directed inward again. I had never before found answers outside myself. One day it occurred to me that I was God. That did not seem entirely unreasonable, after all. Perhaps that is what my history teacher had meant when he said that man had created God. Certainly I was a creator: I created myself, I created my world. Were these not the very attributes of God the Creator? When I say that I created myself, I mean that by active participation in the process of growth and change I directed my own progress. I created my world by the way I chose to see it. I saw things differently from other people, therefore I lived in a different world from them, a world of my own creation. I saw the night as a friend, the stars as lives and the falling stars as genius. I saw school as an aberration of my world. Surely I was my own God.

'The problem with this concept arose because of other people, other people who were more than a figment of my imagination. Other people like the school principal, who one day called me into his office for a chat. He was interested in knowing why I was spending my time down by the riverside and not in class. I explained to him the question I had set myself and the answer I had come up with. He listened quietly and with an unfeigned interest until I ended my discourse with, "So you see, I really am God!"

'He was silent for a few seconds. I figured he was wondering how to address God whom he had accidentally invited into his office. Then he said, "That's very interesting. I have occasionally thought about this same thing." He paused and I bent forward in my chair to better appreciate his conclusions on a subject that held such all-engrossing interest for me. I never denied any man his say in such things. I would not have it said that I was an unjust God. "I have also reached the same conclusion. I think that I am God! Especially here at the school. This is my world and I rule it as I see fit!"

'My forehead wrinkled and my eyebrows grew together. An undisguised "Hmmm" escaped my lips. Was this man trying to usurp the throne of God? Was this a challenge to my Godhead? I looked around the room but it didn't in the least remind me of Olympus where the Gods were supposed to dwell. But I had learned not to be hasty in exposing my thoughts or reactions: I went to class to please him.

'But I sat in the back of the room where the drone of the lectures did not disturb my pondering the situation before me. I had to be reasonable. Selfishness had never solved anything that I knew of. There could be but one answer: if I could come to the conclusion that I was God then so could anyone else who followed the same line of reasoning.

'I was not about to bow myself before any man. I could not admit two Gods in my world. I had no choice but to eliminate both of them. This answer that I had arrived at was simply not practical. I was not God; I was right back where I started from. This question of the existence of God was not going to afford an easy solution.

'Not long after this we moved to northern California and I began my endeavor anew. The beauty of the mountains, the forests, the farms and the sea that lapped at them, colored the course of my pondering. I came to think that perhaps God existed in all things. The giant redwoods and the purple mountains spoke of His Majesty. The great and small plots of fertile land with their thousand shades of tender greens pushing toward life spoke of His Beauty. The roar and surge of the ocean, as cold as it was crashing, spoke of His Power. Even great poetry spoke of God in all things:

> Thou, both End and Origin
> Thou without and Thou within –
> From every eye Thou hidest well,
> And yet in every eye dost dwell.*

'This seemed a most fit solution to the question. I walked around with bright eyes. Everywhere I saw God. "No thing have I perceived, except that I perceived God within it, God before it, or God after it."† If I was not God, at least I was in heaven. Now my peculiar habit of talking to the night fully bloomed. Everywhere I went, at any time, I spoke to the sky, the moon, the land, the sea, the flowers; in everything I saw the image of God. My friends thought I was funny; my family thought I was crazy. I was happy in the presence of God.

'The gradual evolution of all things, however, is to unite. Some people say it is to divide, but those people are simply looking at things upside-down: they've still got their feet firmly planted on the ground when they say this and that is no position to say anything important! Anyway, as was perhaps inevitable, I slowly began to address God as a singular rather than a complexity.

'I resisted this at first. When I found myself walking home from work at night and praying – either in appreciation of the beauty of things or out of my extreme wanting of a car to come by, pick me up, and offer me a ride to my doorstep – I would suddenly stop dead in my tracks and shake my head clear saying, "No! No, Adam. No. Wake up! You don't believe in one Omnipotence. You believe God is everywhere. There is a difference, you know." Then I'd explain the difference to myself, and, to top it off, I'd swear that, even as tired as I was, I wouldn't accept a ride if a car did come by and offer

---

* Rúmí, *The Mathnaví*. Trans. Marzieh Gail.

† A statement attributed to 'Alí ibn Abú Tálib, the son-in-law of Muhammad, as mentioned in the *Kitáb-i-Íqán* of Bahá'u'lláh, p. 102. Previously related by Siyyid Kázim in his *Sharh Khutbih Tutunjiyyih*, by Fayd Káshání in his *Hidden Words*, and by Muhammad Láhijí in his *Sharh Gulshani Ráz*.

me one. How could I accept it? – it would be intellectually dishonest.

'Well, one night I was walking home and I was dead tired. It happened again; I caught myself praying to God – the God I didn't believe in. So I slowly, drowsily, took myself step by step through this process of getting it right. No sooner had I sworn that I wouldn't accept a ride than a Volkswagen pulled up with a college student at the wheel. The last thing I said as I stepped into the car was: "To hell with promises!"

'We talked a bit on the way to my house but I was pretty tired. I had just about enough energy and awareness left to direct him properly and to answer his half-heard questions "yes" or "no". I don't remember all that we were talking about but I do remember one of his questions: he asked if I believed in God. I remember saying that I had tried not to but found that I really didn't have any choice in the matter. That answer must have satisfied him because I don't remember saying anything more before our arriving at my house. I thanked him, got out of the car and stumbled to my bed. I was no longer atheist or pantheist; I was a believer in the One God.'

Adam paused for a few moments and gazed long and hard at the waterfall. It was above us and before us and its mist had enwrapped us. It was a good feeling on a warm day. Then he asked, 'Is this one waterfall or a myriad waters falling? And the pond that seems so whole, is it really that? Aristotle led us a step back for every step forward when he said that a thing cannot be (A) and (not-A) at the same time. That simple statement is a denial of the foremost aspect of reality.' There wasn't anything I could say to these wanderings of his mind so I just watched the place where the waterfall became the pool and waited for him to continue with his story. I didn't have to wait for long.

'I was a believer in the One God. But that's not a thing as simple as it might sound. The concept of the One God has never been quite straight in our minds. Maybe it never will be. When we say one God what we really mean is the One Gods. And when we say the many Gods I don't think that we mean anything more or less than the One God. Look around us now: India is a prime example. This is one of the great seats of religion. She worships the thousand attributes of God as though they were distinct. Is she a monotheistic or a polytheistic nation? You were just saying that the Great Buddha, to whose God all these temples were built, never spoke about God at all. Maybe He thought that there was no point in doing so; we would only get it confused in the end. Well we got it confused anyway! Or Christendom – our own native place – is she as monotheistic as she is said to be? How many Gods do the Christians worship? One? Three? What does it mean: three in one? Can we really be blamed for our misunderstanding of this most central tenet of religion? The concept of God is too far beyond us. We cannot hold God in our petty minds; how can the finite hold the infinite? Books and more books are written about this single question but nothing is ever made clearer. Our hearts will always be troubled by the mention of God. This is the greatest oppression known to man, but at the same time the greatest challenge, the greatest joy! There is not even a proper starting point – where can we begin? Should we first ask what is the human heart? Or what is God? Or who is Christ? Lord! It's wonderful!

'I began my monotheistic endeavors with, "Who is Christ?" Do you remember the words from *Jesus Christ Superstar*? "Jesus Christ, Jesus Christ/ Who are You? What have You sacrificed?/ . . . Who besides Yourself are Your friends at the top?/ Was Buddha where it's at? Was He where You are?/ Did Muhammad move a mountain or was that just PR?/ . . . If You'd come today You would have reached a whole nation . . ."

'*Superstar* became popular about the same time I first began trying to fathom the mystery of Jesus. I would sit for hours and ponder those few words: they held so much. After all, who was Christ? Was He God? God made flesh? Was He a Teacher? Was He a Superman or was He an inspired and elder brother – the First among the sons of God? But don't misunderstand me; for all my searching, and for all my approaching the question from a hundred different angles, I never came one step closer to understanding the central mystery. If I accomplished the least thing it was that I brought myself up to date. I mean to say that after another year or two I stopped asking: "Who is Christ?" and began asking: "Who is Bahá'u'lláh?" We never stop searching because we can never find the answer we seek; if we cannot (honestly) maintain a hope of succeeding in our search, then, at least, we can protect ourselves from despair.

'I attended every different kind of church service. I spent a week floating down a river in Florida with a group of Holy Rollers. When everybody else walked across the street at the sight of a Jehovah's Witness, I ran toward them. I devoured their magazine *The Watchtower* but afterwards my belly was still empty. Truly, I was Majnun sifting the sands. I was mocked for my insistence in such futile search. I cooked many a dinner for Mormon missionaries and read many a chapter of the *Book of Mormon* and was left as empty as before. No one knew who Christ was! They all claimed they did; but no one knew. I learned a lot of fascinating things about Christianity but very little about Christ. I learned to be more dissatisfied than ever; and more hungry than ever. I think that one of the greatest things that bothered me was the insistence that Christ was the only way. He is, but not in the limited way they meant it! Christ said, "I am the way, the truth, and the life: no man cometh unto the Father, but by Me," but Muhammad and Buddha said pretty much the same thing. Jesus also said, "Had ye believed Moses, you would have believed Me." Did this mean that Jesus and Moses taught the same thing? Did it mean that They were essentially One and the same? And Muhammad and Buddha, were they Christs unto their own people? If this were so, and things certainly seemed to point towards it being so, then why did the Christians hate the Muslims, the Muslims hate the Hindus, and everyone hate the Jews? To the fundamentalist Christian mind anyone who did not accept Jesus Christ as his personal savior was doomed to hell; fire and brimstone, devils with bad breath and pointy pitchforks were all in store for these infidels. It did not matter that these people might worship the One God more regularly or with greater austerity and deeper renunciation of the world than the Christians themselves did. It did not matter that they accepted Moses, or Muhammad, or Buddha as Lord, because they were wrong and that's all there was to it! Muhammad and the Buddha? The more tolerant were willing to grant that maybe they were inspired individuals; maybe – if the sun were out, the flowers in bloom, and the baby wasn't crying – maybe. But much more often they were declared anti-Christs, the misleaders of the people, and the destroyers of true religion. Had I known that I was going to get caught in a whirlwind of hatred, intolerance, and fratricide, I might never have asked the question. Where were a people with a wider view? Where were a people who were tolerant of conflicting statements and who accepted other's beliefs? The Christians were right about one thing: we desperately needed Christ to return, and soon. The world is in a terrible state. Religion is a mess. I could imagine a miner's son walking the Kentucky hills who would set minds racing from out their mire of complacency, who would set hearts, now bleeding with love, at peace. Or perhaps He would be an African herdsman whose smile would still armies and whose command would set the world spinning in its orbit. But whoever He was and wherever He came, we needed Him now. "If You'd come today, You would have reached a whole nation . . ."

'But for all my disappointment I didn't stop searching. Early one Sunday morning I went over to Richard's house and shook him out of bed. He grumbled and groaned and asked if I knew it was Sunday. I said I knew. He said that even God sleeps on Sunday. I had never thought of it quite like that before. But I was determined: I got him up and made some breakfast. I had eggs and toast and he had half a box of cornflakes. He always had half a box of cornflakes. Finally, an hour or so later he was fed and showered and at least half dressed. Rubbing his head with a towel he asked, "So why'd you get me up on a Sunday morning?"

'"I thought we'd go to church somewhere. I bought a new suit yesterday."

'"So you did. Suits are a damn sight too imposing if you ask me!"

'"I didn't ask you. I'll ask you about things you know about. Suits you don't know about."

'"So what church did you have in mind. I've got no love for the Mormon; it doesn't give black men the same honors it gives fifteen-year-old white boys. It's too WASPY for my taste. Say, I have never been to a Catholic Mass."

'"I was going to let you decide but let's have it be something new for both of us."

'I suppose he figured that since I had got him out of bed hours earlier than was his wont, we might as well do something interesting. His mood was exactly what it would have been if we were considering going to a movie. He never thought there was really any difference between the churches and the cinemas – both were a show – except that perhaps (if we were lucky) we could get by without paying for the entertainment at a church. "Well, okay. Let's see what's playing," he said as he reached for the telephone book. He began thumbing through the yellow pages of the advertisement section and found the heading: Churches. He scanned the list back to front and read aloud the occasional advertisement or slogan. I had to admit, they sounded theatrical. Occasionally he read out the name of a church but we would discard it because I had already been there, or we'd find it was ten miles out of town, or something. Then he said, "Now here's something. You'll like this; it sounds eastern . . Bahá'í." He stumbled at the word once but then got hold of it. There was no advertisement, just a telephone number. We agreed that the name sounded interesting and that it was new to both of us, so we telephoned. That is, he telephoned; I hated to telephone anyone about anything. Maybe it was a phobia about disembodied voices: I always felt it was impossible to understand what a person was trying to say unless I could see their eyes.

'Richard enjoyed telephoning as much as I hated it. He settled down into an easy chair and began what promised to be a long conversation with the person on the other end of the line. I went into the kitchen and began setting up the chess board. While I simulated a game I kept an ear half open to the telephone conversation. I envied Richard's ability to talk to anyone without stumbling. He got the preliminaries of when and where out of the way early; at that point I would have been at a loss for what to say, but not Richard. He launched right into questions about the tenets of the Faith. At first his questions were about dates and places but soon they took on a philosophical bent. There began long silences when he was listening and long periods when he discoursed on one of his pet philosophies. It was going to be a long Sunday and I had just check-mated myself—it was as if I always knew what I was going to do next — I never could beat myself at that game. Slowly I let the phone conversation fade into the background and concentrated on another variation of the last play that could just possibly lead to a draw. When you're playing against yourself, drawing is winning. Richard, I knew, would give me the details of the conversation only after he had exhausted all the possibilities of discussion or when she (I knew instinctively that it was a she whose voice he had trapped in that inhuman instrument) said straight out that she had other things to do. God help us, I thought, if she liked telephones and philosophy too. She did; but two hours later she did have other things to do. By the time the conversation was over I had lost three games and had fixed lunch. It was ready when Richard came in to enlighten me.

'"What did she have to say? Lunch is ready."

'"Good. Thanks. All that talking made me hungry."

'"Yeh, me too," I said sarcastically.

'"You've got to learn not to be afraid of phones. They don't bite. Anyway, it was worthwhile getting up so early. If we had called now she wouldn't have been there. How did you know it was a woman?'

'"Lucky guess," I said smiling. "What did she say?"

'"She said it was not Christian, or Jewish or Muslim. So there was no weekly service as such. But she invited us to a fireside – nice word, huh; it kind of reminds you of Franklin Delano – on Wednesday night at seven-thirty. Not far from here either. Can you be free on Wednesday?"

'"I'm scheduled to work but I can arrange something. How old was she?"

'"About as old as Franklin Delano, I guess. Interesting lady though."

'"Yeh, so what was all the heavy philosophy?"

'He spent all of lunch and two games of chess relating the information he had solicited from the woman, expanding on it with the odd flourish. I won both games: they were no contest – he was too busy talking. Then we put the chess set away and got down a volume of the encyclopedia. We looked up Bahá'í and Bábí and <u>Shi</u>'ah Islam and learned a great deal more. The more we read the more excited I became. The whole thing was fascinating: the birth of a new Faith, the slaughter of its adherents, and its continued spread solely on the merits of its principles and the dedication of the believers. Richard tried the phone again in the middle of the afternoon and, had the woman been home, he probably would have stayed on the phone until nightfall. But she wasn't home and so, with our initial curiosities satisfied, we settled down for a Sunday matinee on television.

'I was able to exchange workshifts with someone else at the Pizza parlor on Wednesday and so came directly to Richard's house after school. We had a fine home-cooked meal which his mother had prepared – mashed potatoes and everything – and then walked the mile or so to the address Richard had been given over the phone. That first meeting was interesting – slides of the Holy Land if I recall correctly – but not to the extent as to attract Richard to another; but, then, religion really wasn't to his taste. I, however, was fascinated by the people. They were the reason I came back. There was nothing alike, except their Faith, about any two of them. There was a short, long-haired quiet Viet Nam veteran lodging with a lanky, talkative metallurgist. There was an old woman, crippled and half-blind, and her grand-daughter, who couldn't have been more than seventeen and who sat on the floor beside her chair, her head on the old woman's lap. There was a black woman married to a white man, both middle-aged, who lived in a nearby town. There were four or five other students of various hues and nationalities. They referred to themselves as a flower garden, and it was more than an apt expression: it was a beautiful reality. There was a definite aura of love like the perfume that arises from a rose garden. This is what I saw; Richard was not enchanted as I was. It's too bad, I wish he could have seen those people the way I did – if it was rose-colored glasses that I wore, I would have gladly taken them off and given them to him.

'I continued to go to the Wednesday night meetings even after they were transferred to another apartment complex halfway across town. The meetings that began at seven-thirty often lasted until midnight. Many of the people who came went back to their homes at a reasonable hour, but those few of us who had a lot to say and a lot to hear, talked and argued and told stories late into the night. During the nine months that I continued to attend these firesides I thought the reason I went was because they were a group of people who had the capacity to speak about a subject as inflammable as religion with both intelligence and humor. I know now that the reason I was so strongly attracted was because they loved me.

'They had no qualms about listening to diverse points of view nor did they try to prove their view right by degrading mine or any other's. They were a people whom it felt good to be with, good to share my deepest questions with.

'I still saw the Mormon missionaries and the Jehovah's Witnesses and anyone else whose path I happened to run across. I often spoke to them about the view and attitude that the Bahá'ís took on a given subject. Although I was often not in full agreement with the Bahá'í philosophies, I was distressed when some other denomination spoke disparagingly of them. When this happened, it was not the Bahá'í philosophies that I began to reconsider, but those of their more or less hostile adversaries. I suppose that this was one of the prime reasons that I grew to accept, in ever greater degree, the Bahá'í views. Undoubtedly one of the saddest things about Christianity is that there are hundreds of denominations, fractions and sects, and few of them will humble themselves to the point of speaking with admiration, or even kindliness, of each other. Christianity exudes disunity and discord. The Bahá'ís wore the refreshing scent of unity and amenity. They accepted the divine missions of Moses, Jesus, Muhammad, Buddha, Zoroaster, Krishna and certain others without hateful bickering. The acceptance of these Prophets was a basic tenet of their faith.

'The discussions at the Bahá'í firesides usually centered around one or another of the basic principles of the Cause. One week we might discuss the unity of God; another time someone might speak of universal peace or world government. The discussion might revolve around the need of education for all the world's children, or the elimination of religious, racial, national and class prejudices, or the need for each individual to be freely given and to freely take the responsibility of investigating truth independently and for himself. I often spent my hours pondering the many aspects of these proposals. Sometimes I could hardly wait until the next Wednesday to discuss my thoughts.

'But too, sometimes I felt just the opposite. If I had been like a measuring rod by which my friends were measured, I felt now as though I was measured by the concepts of these people. There were times that I remember quickly stepping behind pillars or around corners because a Bahá'í was approaching and I felt as though I had a mean heart or a weak mind. I could not face them. They seemed not only to measure me but to push and propel me.

'Then came one afternoon in April when the sun was full and the birds rejoicing at the arrival of spring. The cherry blossoms carpeted the quiet residential roads with the color of snow and the fragrance of flowers. It seemed as though it was the King of Days. I walked slowly along the streets weaving a trail through the blossoms, nothing on my mind to speak of but happiness and the quiet rejoicing in a wonderful day, until, suddenly, I was stopped in my meanderings and stood in the middle of a vision. All of a sudden I had noticed that the birds were singing – not only some of the birds, but all of them, each and every one – and that they were singing in chorus as though they were one. Then the trees and the blossoms drifting down were also singing. I turned a full circle, lost in utter rapture, and found that every living thing, including the very earth on which I walked, was singing. It was a hymn of praise and happiness and rejoicing. I wanted badly to join in but my mouth could not utter a sound. Finally, a croak burst forth from my breaking lungs as I tried to join the chorus. But my croaking closed that world to me and suddenly all was silent. I had tried but had been found unworthy to join in the song. I was crest-fallen and sat down on the curb to rest and regather my courage.

'I walked the streets of Eureka all that afternoon and night puzzling over why I had been counted unworthy. I walked until long past midnight and my legs could walk no farther. Next I knew I was on my knees, alone in the middle of a small park. There were the boughs of a fir tree and the sparkling lights of Orion above my outstretched arms. There were tears on my cheeks and my voice still croaked though I beseeched the stars to intercede in my behalf. "O God! Make me worthy. Recreate me as Thou would have me be!" I was in a terrible pain like the oppression of carrying a heavy weight.

'When I awoke the next morning I went into my garden. It was a Wednesday. As I turned over the grass and the loam and marked out the boundaries of the garden the sweat rolled off me and joined with the earth. My mind was as active as my body. Both worked at a feverish pace as though to shake off a fever. I remembered a few weeks before when I had some extra money – about fifty dollars – and I wanted to offer it to the Bahá'ís as a contribution. They would not accept it; more than that, they could not accept it. One of them explained that only Bahá'ís could contribute to Bahá'í funds as it was considered a privilege and an honor to contribute toward the building of a new world order.

'I told myself again and again that I was a loner and had never joined any organization, that I saw more clearly and understood better by standing outside of groups like this. So why trouble myself about it? This was just another organization that would limit my freedom with its restrictions. But these were good people with high ideals and it would be an honor to be counted one of them. My goal was to rid myself of my lesser nature, to become selfless; and that was a personal endeavor. I vowed to myself that if I were ever able to tear away the veils of selfishness, then I would become a Bahá'í. Then I would be worthy and ready. I was satisfied with this decision; I was also finished with the day's work in the garden.

'Later that same night I went to the Bahá'í fireside. A Persian Bahá'í had come from San Francisco and spoke about a variety of things. But the part of his talk that struck my interest was a story about a friend of his. This friend was an old man and had been a

Baptist all of his life. His parents had been Baptists before him. He knew a great deal about the Bahá'í Faith and he believed in the divinity of Bahá'u'lláh. But he had not and would not become a Bahá'í.

'He went on to talk about tradition and how sometimes it can become a prison chain that secures us and binds us, that keeps us from the freedom of individual initiative and expression. All this was fine and good but it didn't apply to me; I was more interested in the old man: I asked why it was not enough that the old man believed in Bahá'u'lláh. Why did he have to become a Bahá'í too? I identified with that old man. The Persian was not slow with his answer, nor was he hesitant. He said that today the world was in a dire state and that it needed to be redirected and revived. No single individual could comprehend the extent of the problem nor could he do anything but exhaust himself in single combat with such an enormous beast. Yet still it was our responsibility to change the world, to redirect its course; we could only do this by changing the hearts of its peoples. Only a community – a community directed by divine guidance and enlisting divine assistance – had any hope of succeeding at such an endeavor. As individuals we were nothing, he said, but as a community we were strong through our unity and our resolve.

'His answer was good but it demanded some thought before I accepted it. He went on with his talk and a number of other questions were asked, but I was half oblivious to it all. I sat back in a corner of the room and pondered this answer. An hour or more had probably passed before I arose and went to a friend – a Bahá'í whom I respected and loved – to ask if he could show me anywhere in Bahá'u'lláh's own writings where it was said that a person should become a Bahá'í. He was preparing to take someone home but he paused for a few minutes to rummage through a bookcase. He finally chose a copy of the *Kitáb-i-Aqdas*, turned to the first passage in it, and handed it to me saying, "Read this carefully and if you have any questions I'll return in forty-five minutes." The passage explained the twin duties of man: first to recognize the Manifestation of God in this day – the actual phrasing is much more beautiful than that . . . let me see if I can remember it exactly: "The first duty prescribed by God for His servants is the recognition of Him Who is the Dayspring of His Revelation and the Fountain of His laws, Who representeth the Godhead in both the Kingdom of

His Cause and the world of creation . . . It behoveth every one who reacheth this most sublime station, this summit of transcendent glory, to observe every ordinance of Him Who is the Desire of the world. These twin duties are inseparable. Neither is acceptable without the other. Thus hath it been decreed by Him Who is the Source of Divine Inspiration.”

'Beautiful, isn't it? I went back to my corner to read that passage and what immediately followed. I read it slowly to be sure that I had not misconstrued some word or phrase. Finally I realized I had no choice. At the same time I realized something else: the solution to my problem in the garden that morning dawned on me. From out of nowhere I finally understood that my very isolation and individualism, my pride in calling myself a loner, was the next veil I needed to tear away. I knew it was not the last veil, nor anywhere near it, but it was definitely the next.

'Not only had I no choice in what I was about to do, but I rejoiced in that very lack of liberty. I have always believed that greater understanding limits choice rather than increases it (as most people seem to think). One of my personal challenges was to learn to radiantly acquiesce to these self-imposed limitations.

'My joy has always been of the quiet kind, so quietly and unobtrusively I went over to another Bahá'í – Elaine, the woman whose apartment we were in – and told her that if she could find a Bahá'í declaration card, then I was ready to sign it. Her eyes widened and brightened and a smile took command of her face from ear to ear. With all my arguments and objections I think that she had lost hope that I would ever reach that point. She must have thought of me as a prodigal son returned home because rather than getting the card as I suggested she enwrapped me in her arms and pulled me to her breast. She was a strong woman and not only could I not free myself from this unexpected development but I couldn't breathe either. She had let out a cry of surprise and joy as she pulled me to her and its very unexpectedness had scared the breath right out of me. As she held me I struggled to find some way to breathe; there wasn't any. When she finally released me I was beet-red with embarrassment and lack of oxygen. The words of resignation were still unfinished in my mind: "Well, Adam, this is it. Your time has come. But what a way to go . . . funny, I always thought that these moments were supposed to bring new life, not . . ." Suddenly I was free again – half dead, but free – I gulped down a breath of air and began to cough on it. Elaine left me supported by someone else while she went to get the declaration card.

'By the time she returned I had recovered enough to be able to read the card and put my name to it; but I still didn't really have my breath and the room had suddenly become very hot. I knew I needed to get outside and into the air. My head was swimming and only the cold spring air would clear it. I got to the door and made to go out; I was on the stairwell landing when a voice called from the kitchen, "Where are you going so early?" It was the voice of the man from San Francisco.

'I turned around to answer him, still walking – but backwards now, "I need fresh air and time to think. I've got to walk down the stairs before . . ." As I walked backwards my feet came into contact with a cardboard box. Suddenly my little world began to spin and I began to tumble. I had just enough control to finish my sentence, ". . . before I fall down them!" I tumbled and slid down two flights of stairs and finally lay sprawled on the ground at their bottom. The outer door was open and a wave of spring hit me like a bucket of cold water. I got up mumbling. "I'm okay, I'm okay; I just need to walk a bit." The last thing I saw was the people lined along the balcony, some laughing, some worried, as I walked out the door and into the night with which I was so familiar.'

Book II
YOUTH
Being the next six years of Adam's life

Rejoice, O young man, in thy youth; and let thy heart cheer thee in the days of thy youth, and walk in the ways of thine heart, and in the sight of thine eyes: but know thou, that for all these things God will bring thee into judgement. Therefore remove sorrow from thy heart, and put away evil from thy flesh; for childhood and youth are vanity.

Ecclesiastes 11:9–10

Go east of your dreaming form
Let peace and silence spin your yarn.
What harm can befall thee
In yon wilderness of clove?

Go east of ginger trees,
Go soft and silent like the breeze.
With ease be off and wander
In yon wilderness of clove.

Go home past the goldenrods
Where fools and angels lose their odds.
And Gods of our ancestors
Did immerse themselves in clove.

Go on toward the Crimson Shore,
Beyond this life of metaphor
Where doors of Understanding's
House decorates them with clove.

Be lions roaring in the forests of knowledge,
Whales swimming in the oceans of life.
Prepare to meet Bahá'u'lláh
In the Garden of Clove.

Seals and Crofts, 'East of Ginger Trees'

CHAPTER I

Being how Adam searches for faith as a goatherd, a scholar, a carpenter and a missionary

And Joseph was thirty years old when he stood before Pharaoh king of Egypt. And Joseph went out from the presence of Pharaoh and went throughout all the land of Egypt. And in the seven plenteous years the earth brought forth by handfuls. And he gathered up all the food of the seven years, which were in the land of Egypt, and laid up the food in the cities: the food of the field, which was round about every city, laid he up in the same. And Joseph gathered corn as the sand of the sea, very much, until he left numbering; for it was without number. And unto Joseph were born two sons before the years of famine came, which Asenath the daughter of Potipherah priest of On bare unto him. And Joseph called the name of the firstborn Manasseh: For God, said he, hath made me forget all my toil, and all my father's house. And the name of the second called he Ephraim: For God hath caused me to be fruitful in the land of my affliction.

Genesis 41:46–52

I

Adam checked his billfold again. Inside were twenty-two dollars in food stamps and a five-dollar bill. It was enough; only a few months before he had traveled to Mexico City and back on twenty dollars. He replaced the billfold in his front pants pocket and then raised his hand to his left breast to be sure that his passport and his traveler's checks were also where they were supposed to be. Diana had carefully sewn a hidden, yet comfortable, pocket into each of his shirts. It was her last gift.

All his affairs were settled. Although he hadn't attended his classes since he returned from Mexico, he had gone to the school and officially signed out. His garden, just beginning to sprout into a tender green, he had left in the capable hands of a Vietnamese refugee who lived a few houses away. He had quietly taken leave of Diana, of Richard, and of the Bahá'ís whom he had so recently agreed to journey with.

All was in order. His single bag was packed. The room was bare and all the papers gone. Perhaps he had work waiting in France; he had the visas that he needed and the visas he only thought he needed. He had enjoyed preparing for the trip and yet he was not entrapped by a schedule. He was wiser than that: he had traveled before. He had prepared options and possible opportunities but not commitments, he carried addresses and not appointments. He did not know where the journey might lead – it led away and that was enough.

It was May. It was dawn and the sun was on the verge of rising. He walked to the town limits and looked back at Eureka. It was not far from his attic apartment and he had wanted to walk rather than begin hitch-hiking too soon. As he looked at the still sleeping town he unconsciously brushed the dust from off his shirt and pants. It wasn't until much later that he would realize the symbolism of that act. Never again would he return to Eureka as people returned home. He would visit again from time to time but he would feel like a visitor.

Then he turned to the east and squinted into the sun. The main four-lane highway was another mile down the road. He could hear the traveling sounds – the crickets, the wind on the long grass and the rush of the distant cars – as he began to walk. These sounds had never left him.

Five days later he was in a hammock over-looking the course of the Hudson River as it passed through a National Park some eighty miles out of New York City. He had already been in the city and confirmed a plane reservation to Paris. He lay back in his hammock and began to read, but only a few lines, before his mind began to drift again, from California to Paris and to all the places between. His had been a full five days. There was the day spent sitting in the middle of the new interstate highway in the middle of the barren piece of wind-swept rock they called Wyoming. 'What a God-forsaken place!' he thought, and shivered at the thought. In the fourteen hours he sat there only three cars had passed. Finally, the last of them – probably more out of curiosity than anything else – had given him a lift. For fourteen hours there was nothing but the

piercing wind, the equally deserted rail line that paralleled the
highway, and the hitch-hikers' epitaphs carved into the cement.
One read: 'I'd rather have a bottle in front of me than a frontal
lobatomy.' And the other was styled after journal entries: 'March
14: Today we have arrived from Fayetteville, Louisiana. March 17:
No food for two days, no cars for three days. March 19: I ate my
partner yesterday. Still no ca . . .' The epitaphs fit Wyoming; Adam
had wondered if he was ever going to get out of there.

Eventually he did. He got to Blue Earth, Minnesota, and a
downpour at midnight. But Blue Earth at midnight in a rainstorm
was the last place he wanted to be. So he said a prayer he had recently
learned and which seemed appropriate to the situation.

> Is there any Remover of difficulties save God? Say:
> Praised be God! He is God! All are His servants,
> and all abide by His bidding!*

It was a fine prayer and a car came by and gave him a lift not five
minutes later. Adam had no idea whether the prayer actually had
anything to do with the car and he really didn't want to know. But
he did know that the moment he stepped into that car he was swept
with a wave of guilt at having said the prayer at all: maybe it hadn't
really been raining that hard after all!

Later there was the born-again Christian who had gone a
hundred miles and a full afternoon out of his way to take him to the
Bahá'í House of Worship in Wilmette, Illinois. He had seen
Toronto again after eight years and New York after three. Soon he
would be in Paris. 'And how can you keep the boys on the farm once
they have seen Gay Paree?' he said half-aloud, then thought: Paris
prices will probably make me leave for the farms pretty quickly.
And he glanced down at the book again.

2

Adam was reading the Bible, reading of Joseph's rise and fall in the
world of affairs. He had chosen the books he carried with him
carefully. He had brought the *Bible* (King James Version), the
Kitáb-i-Aqdas (The Book of Laws), *The Seven Valleys and the Four
Valleys* (the book of travels) and *The Hidden Words* (the Essence of
Religion). France wasn't envisioned as a vacation or an escape but as
* Revealed by Siyyid 'Alí Muḥammad, The Báb.

a retreat and a reorientation. A part of his life was past and a new part beginning: Adam wanted an insight into where he had been and into where he was going. These four books and the rolling hills beneath the Pyrenees were to be his companions.

He had joined the Bahá'í community; he was no longer a loner responsible only to and for himself. But he did not yet understand community life or the ways of a community member. He was drawn to these hills to ponder just these questions and to discover their answers. He had come alone . . . this was to be his last sojourn into the world alone. There was precedent for his decision in every story. From Moses to Bahá'u'lláh, each went alone into the mountains and the deserts to commune with God, and each was made stronger and greater for it. Adam was no Moses but undisturbed communion was good for all the sons of God.

Adam saw Paris, but for him, then, it was no more than New York with another name. He had stayed long enough to be repelled by the ugliness of the Eiffel Tower and to secure a job in the southern hills. He was to be a goatherd for the next six months at a small family farm that was equidistant from Spain and from the sea. Both were ever with him during his stay in that country: the mountains of Spain silently overshadowed his days and the unheard crashing of breakers on the rocks chastened his nights. The couple whose goats he tended were old and kind. They gave him a small cottage built of rock and tile and hand-hewn beams. He could not speak with them, but together, in silence, they ate and enjoyed the meals that the old woman prepared.

Everyone had their own responsibilities. The old woman cooked, and baked and cared for the potato patch. The old man fished with a net in the nearby lake, and arranged that the goat's milk got to the milk plant in town and the necessary provisions got back. They all arose at five a.m. and milked the goats before they sat down to cheese and bread and coffee at seven. Directly after finishing Adam took his cane and his hat, and his rubber boots if it had rained the night before, and began to drive the goats along the road to the sea. But they never reached the sea; instead they hopped and hobbled and pranced around the hills and through the neighbors' pastures – through gates left open and wire fences left unmended for them (because the old couple had no sons) – until they reached the rocky, grass pasture with ancient, gnarled, oak trees on which the goats rubbed the hairy patch of scalp between their horns. The trees had no bark below the meter mark because the goats had rubbed them bare; it didn't matter because no one who lived nearby owned the land or saw the naked trees.

Adam lay beneath his favorite tree, his head and back against a boulder left ages ago by the retreating ice, and watched the goats scratch and play and fight. There were some fifty she-goats and three or four bucks. Each had its own personality and character: some were fighters, some gamesters, most young, some old. One got caned a dozen times a day for going where he wasn't supposed to; another was fat, stupid and half-blind, and always got stuck between the same two trees. The young bucks were always trying to mount a she-goat but were most often frustrated by the gnashing teeth of the female or the charge of the jealous old billy that ruled the realm. There were two or three bell-wearers, who would come up to Adam and butt him until he scratched their heads himself. Sometimes he would grab their horns and they would jerk their heads and kick their feet until he couldn't hold them any longer. Then they would prance back to their grazing and he would return to gazing at the road that wound along far below or to meditating on the sentences of the book he carried with him.

Adam usually took the Bahá'í books with him during the day because they were lighter to carry and because they carried the greater promise of things to ponder. They were more mystical. The Bible became a book for reading after the evening meal in the front room of the old couple's home. They liked the fact that he was reading the Bible from cover to cover and often asked him to read aloud while they knitted and stoked the fire. Neither of them could understand a word of English but they seemed to enjoy the intonation and song in his voice. Occasionally the old man would don his ancient, plastic-rimmed spectacles and bring down the old, dusty French Bible from its place on the mantel and read along silently as Adam read aloud. The old woman, if she had ever learned to read, had long since forgotten again. She had no need to read. She knitted along contentedly.

There were no Bahá'ís in any part of that region and so Adam was given a certain respite before joining a Bahá'í community. During the months alone he read and re-read the Book of Laws, and he pondered the book's application, its meaning and its import. The laws were, most definitely, the laws of an ideal, God-fearing, God-directed society. Most were very much out of place today – they simply could not be understood in today's context. But slowly they were being implemented. Slowly the people of the world would evolve to understanding and obedience. Nothing that was good, or lasting, or solid, was built overnight. A strong base takes time and dedication to construct, and a strong base is essential for the coming into being of the pyramid's point. The laws were good, but the purpose behind the laws was great. The pyramid was a wonder, but where it pointed was the greater wonder.

> Think not that We have revealed unto you a mere
> code of laws. Nay, rather, We have unsealed the
> choice Wine with the fingers of might and power.
> To this beareth witness that which the Pen of
> Revelation hath revealed. Meditate upon this, O
> men of insight!

Adam prayed. He learned to pray after the Bahá'í manner. There were three obligatory prayers of which he was supposed to choose one to say each day. They were of varying length and each was beautiful. He could not choose between them and so didn't; he said all three daily. He committed each one to memory along with its own pattern of genuflections and risings. He rejoiced in saying these prayers because they were as much poetry as prayer and held allusions that ran through cultures and dispensations and through his own heart to his God. They were milk from the breast of God and he was like the new-born babe held close.

Through these quiet months, through these prayers and meditations alone in the hills before his God, Adam began to cleanse his heart of the dross of lesser cravings and lesser opinions. He grew to prepare himself for the journey ahead, a journey on which one foot would only infrequently stand beside the other, a journey through half-life and in half-light. His journey was to be at the earliest dawn of day when sleep still inhabits the eyes and the meaning of life is but half-awake. The journey would not be an easy one.

Half-light became dramatically clear when Adam went to Marseilles for two weeks and met a woman. She lived in the room across from the one which he rented. They sat and talked in their broken accents until late into the evenings. Neither her mind nor his was on the talking, but on each other. When the situation could go no further in that vein, she arose one evening and took Adam by the hand toward her bedroom. But Adam stopped at the threshold and could not go in. He looked at her hand in his, her arm, her long black hair that was not French, and into her eyes. It had already gone much too far; he would see that hand, those eyes in his dreams for a thousand nights to come. It would be a long torment if he did not enter the room and a long torment if he did. He closed his eyes, took a long draught of air to relieve his seduced heart; 'I cannot,' he said, 'there is tomorrow.' And he turned and left her there.

Soon summer was past and winter's clouds began to threaten. The grass was cut and in the silo, the fences were mended, the potatoes had been dug up and put into the cellar. The she-goats began to grow fat with young and Adam decided it was time to leave France. The goats, the hills and the old man with plastic glasses had given him the strength to face the pains and problems of life within a community. Without these quiet months of meditation and work he would not have been able to remain or grow as a community member.

3

After a brief visit to Eureka in late December, Adam went to Las Cruces, New Mexico. He traveled south with a group of friends. The trip together was good and there was a pulling at Adam's heart when he left them at Los Angeles and turned east, this time to college. He loved to travel more than he loved anything in this world and it was a sacrifice to part with friends going south. But he felt it would be wrong to deny himself the opportunity of higher studies. He was not quite sure why this was so, but nothing is ever lost by taking chances if you know that you are taking chances. Adam knew it. He knew a number of confusing things: that he had not profited by formal schooling since the second grade, that this was a good school and that he had chosen it himself over a year before, that he would be studying for studying's sake alone. If he completed this four-year course he would be no more prepared to hold a respectable job or to make respectable money at that time than he was right then; he took a perverse kind of proud satisfaction from this knowledge. The one thing that he might gain would be an understanding of the philosopher's perspective of western civilization for the last three thousand years. The school was a risk but that was exactly what attracted Adam to it. It was a small, almost unknown, college on the outskirts of Las Cruces. Only two years before (because of funding problems) it had become affiliated with, and loosely attached to, the otherwise conservative and modern state university system of New Mexico. But it had fought to maintain the independence of its forum and perspective. And to a large degree it had succeeded . . . thus far.

The Bahá'í community of Las Cruces, which Adam quickly sought out, abundantly displayed the variety and color of the people of New Mexico. There were Anglos from the north, Chicanos from the south, and Indians who sprang from the center itself. There was a black man from Georgia who was doing a Master's degree at the university. In all, the community numbered about thirty souls. It had been established just after the Second World War when a wounded and disillusioned veteran came with his wife (who was a Bahá'í) from Massachusetts to resettle in Las Cruces. Slowly it had grown in numbers, and slowly and painfully it had grown strong. In the early sixties a dozen Covenant-breakers – Bahá'ís who had broken rank – had settled in Santa Fé, but soon their in-fighting and factionalism threw them to a dozen different corners of the state. If they did not succeed in causing any division in the ranks of the Faith, they did make a lot of noise, and, as a result, the Bahá'í community of Las Cruces was strong within itself, but not outside of itself. Many times it hesitated to have any kind of public proclamation or gathering for fear that some lone Covenant-breaker would show up and a mess would ensue. It had happened before and the community had some right to be hesitant.

But Adam was young and eager and ready to take on the world – alone if necessary – he wasn't hesitant about anything. When he first arrived in Las Cruces and went to the telephone book to call the Bahá'ís he found himself faced with two numbers, apparently two communities. He debated a long time about which one to use. It was at first a confusing, then an exciting dilemma. Finally he let simplicity and synchrony play their rightful part – he had only one dime and only that listed simply as 'The Bahá'í Faith' was a local number. After greetings and all such he told the person on the other end of the line of his interest in calling the second number also. At this there was a noticeable change in the woman's voice and she immediately invited him to consult with the Local Spiritual Assembly on the following night. Adam agreed to meet her the next evening at seven o'clock.

His meeting with the Local Spiritual Assembly was the first in a long series of productive but often painful meetings. Assemblies must discipline the spirit of youth without demoralizing or crushing it. Sometimes they succeed, as the Local Spiritual Assembly of Las Cruces succeeded with Adam's education. He was their headache for a year and a half; they were his heartache. Together they grew to love one another.

After welcoming Adam into the community they began to explain about the community's history, particularly with reference to the Covenant-breakers. They were open and honest with him. Their frankness with a newcomer amazed him and unhesitatingly claimed his respect. They told the history, the crux of the problem, they produced the letters from the National Spiritual Assembly and the Universal House of Justice concerning the situation. They asked him to read carefully the Will and Testament of 'Abdu'l-Bahá (for it spoke to this matter) before he made any attempt to contact the Covenant-breakers. They told him very bluntly of the danger involved both to himself – his own spiritual growth – and to the community, if he still chose to do this. All this was spoken of with wisdom and courage (as one or two of the people were visibly shaken even at the discussion of the matter). But the strength of the Assembly came across most clearly when they finally said that ultimately this choice, like all choices, was his own. With this last they confronted reality head-on rather than barking like a dog that cannot bite or hiding as an ostrich hides its head in the sand. The choice was Adam's and it should not and could not be taken from him. The Assembly had not tried to frighten him, nor had it used any low or dishonest tactic which might have been used. Instead, they spoke with him intimately and honestly, and correctly evaluated his character. As long as the choice was his he would not endanger himself or the community by taking it. Respect for the institution was firmly established at this first meeting.

This was only the beginning of Adam's education in community life. A number of times during the next eighteen months he would be called before the Assembly to explain some one of his un-numbered flights of fancy, or he would challenge the Assembly on some decision or policy. Adam was beginning to grow up and he went through, and caused others to go through, all the pains of growing up.

The college that Adam attended, for example, was a small

community in itself. It was a foolish community of proud misfits; it was a community of artists, intellectuals, malcontents, drug addicts, lovers and other displaced persons. Adam fitted well within this foolishness. He was selfish as a child is selfish: selfish because he did not understand the rights of others, especially in those things that were personal to him. He did what he wanted to do because he did it only to himself. He was irresponsible. Once he had a friend shave his head, first after the fashion of the Mohawk, but then (because his friend, the barber from Mexico, could not cut a straight line) he decided that some other fashion was needed. He had his friend shave all but a round patch high on the back of his head. With that, Adam thought, he could have the benefits of both short and long hair. As his hair grew he would keep it all short but this patch which he would begin to braid. Slowly it would grow into a revised version of the old Chinese braid. What Adam chose to do to himself, what right had anyone to mind? None, perhaps; but no one, not even in a community of artists, was going to allow him that much freedom. It was the fact that Adam did not know this that made his peculiar haircut an irresponsible act.

In less than twenty-four hours Adam's new fashion (apparently much, much bolder than merely shaving one's head) set off waves of talk and silences: his instructors' jaws dropped open when he entered his classes; the cafeteria grew silent when he approached the serving line; and one particularly odious redhead began to dance along beside him chanting: 'Hari, Hari; Krishna, Krishna; Hari Krishna, Hari Krishna . . .' The style Adam selected was, apparently, something close to that worn by the ochre-robed converts to Hinduism who had lately been dancing in the streets of the major cities. It was, also, nearing spring – about the time of the year that they shaved their heads that way.

This, combined with the usual dress Adam wore – a robe made of soft cotton in traditional Navajo colors, mirror sunglasses, and a pair of slippers that his father had given him so long before that they had to be held together with electrical wrapping tape – confused anyone who tried to make any sense out of him.

> Here come old Flat top
> He come grooving up slowly
> He got joo joo eyeball
> He one holy roller

He got hair down to his knee.
Got to be a joker he just do what he please.
. . . .

He say I know you, you know me.
One thing I can tell you is you got to be free.
Come together right now over me . . .*

He was once approached by adherents of the Hindu sect and asked about the temple he belonged to (they asked with an air of reproach about his robe) and he had to explain that he had never met a member of that sect until that very moment. There grew to be a hundred headaches of pride because he stood out from the crowd so completely. The Local Spiritual Assembly strongly suggested that he give up these things and change his manner, reminding him of the law of Bahá'u'lláh not to make oneself a plaything for the idle tongues of the foolish. They also reminded him of the more concrete law about not shaving one's head. The Western Bahá'ís were not bound by these or most of the laws in the *Kitáb-i-Aqdas*, but the Assembly reminded him none-the-less. Somewhat sadly, but obediently, he gave away his coat of many colors. He did not retape his slippers when they next fell apart. He did not cut his growing braid for a number of months, but by summertime he had begun to realize how very selfish a hairstyle it was. With this as a final self-imposed argument he again cut his hair to a more respectable fashion. No longer did the students or faculty tend to confuse the Bahá'í Faith with Hinduism. Now they had to find some other reason to confuse it. The Assembly heaved a sigh of relief and Adam learned to obey. He also learned that obedience to law and counsel could, in a certain – but sure – way, give him a greater degree of liberty. Obedience had, in this case, released him from the idle gossip of weak minds and weak hearts. Just as knowledge and understanding is a part of faith, so is obedience.

4

It was a good school; in its way, perhaps one of the best in the country, but it was not for Adam. Later he would realize that he had not been disciplined enough for its particular curriculum and that

* Lennon/McCartney, 'Come Together'.

125

that was a major cause of his leaving. But there was another reason too: each of the great books had begun to say the same thing: stop reading and go out and discover the secrets and mysteries of life firsthand; go poke into the anthills; go question the revolution of the stars for yourself.

A scholar must apply himself to his books – that is, those books that earlier scholars have designated as worthy – and, although Adam loved to read, he could not do this. When the books became mere words on printed pages he set them aside; while others were studying Greek or memorizing Euclid's theorems, he went west to the Navajo nation to dance and feast on slaughtered sheep. Adam was an utter failure as a scholar.

But each person must find his niche in life and his role in the advancement of civilization. Adam thought long and deep about what he should do. He prayed about it. Finally he decided to join the Carpenters' Union and learn that trade. So he joined the organization, took the classes, and found himself a job until the union could get him one. He began to take pride in the skills he learned and in the tools of the trade. He learned to distinguish between a well-balanced hammer and a poorly-balanced one, between the kinds of handsaws by the alignment of their teeth. He learned to hang doors and to drywall; he learned framing, decking and finishing. He learned to drive a sixteen-pound nail through pine in three blows, through oak in four. He learned that a carpenter needed a beerbelly or suspenders in order to hold up his toolbelt and nail pouches. Adam bought suspenders. When there were no union jobs available, he went non-union and learned to pour concrete and make adobe, to dig ditches and set windows, to plane lumber, read blueprints and install solar heating systems.

But, for all he learned, he was not satisfied; often he was not happy. Just as he had not felt at home with the scholarly in their ivory towers, concocting their wizard's formulas, so too he was not at home with the working man with nine children who swore a blue streak and who needed coarse jokes and a couple of beers after work before he faced the too fertile wife he wished he'd never married. He usually didn't want to see the kids until they were grown, and thoroughly inebriated himself on Friday night before he had to spend his weekend near them. This man was Adam's daily companion, but often only Adam's silence kept him from revealing his disgust. This was the man who the communists believed could change the world. Adam couldn't see it. He only saw a drunk and disillusioned father of nine equally disillusioned kids.

Adam also had problems with the union. They wanted his vote. To ask this implied that the union wanted his freedom of individual thought, individual action. Adam would not sell his vote, but he would not use it either. He had never believed in the system and he was not about to start now, especially when it meant being less than he was. In a dark room, should a candle be snuffed out because the lamps have no oil?

Adam began to question why he had joined the union in the first place rather than simply working outside it. He would learn the same skills, probably more skills, if he went non-union. As he analyzed his original decision he realized that it was nothing more than the security of a union card that had attracted him. That piece of paper that legally defined his relationship to an organization (a piece of paper that could be revoked without reason or explanation) had deceived him by claiming to be security and status. He was somebody doing something when he had that card in his pocket. There was protection, the card told him, against a world that would not believe he was anybody or worthy of doing anything. All that the union wanted in return was that he believe and say what union members should believe and say. The card would guarantee him a job he liked at a better wage every year. He could marry and raise a family if he wanted, without worry. They would all be safe from the evils of society because he held a union card. The funny thing was that his high school counselors had said exactly the same thing about a high school diploma – Adam never got one and found he never needed one either – and then later, others gave exactly the same arguments for getting a college education. But he had discovered that it was wrong to do what was not right for him. It was wrong to become learned if a person didn't love learning. It was wrong to travel if he didn't love traveling, wrong to do a work he didn't love. To be of benefit to society a person must do what he does because he loves to do it. Nothing else is of benefit. Nothing else is secure.

Security, Adam found, is not in having a job with a pay increase every year. It is not in being related to a group of men. It is not in having enough money to supply every want and desire. All these things are essentially evanescent and without substance. Jobs are lost or become dissatisfying. Men die. Banks fail. And desires increase.

Security is almost unknown today. It is certainly misunderstood. The need for security is not a physical need and so cannot be fulfilled by something physical like a house or a job. Each need, he decided, must find its fulfillment in its own realm. Thirst is a physical need and so finds relief or fulfillment through water, a physical element. The need for security is a spiritual thirst; only the spiritual can relieve and fulfill it. A person's security is ultimately linked to his faith in God. Paradoxically, security is found only in the most hidden of hidden entities, only with the most unknown of essences, only within oneself:

> And if thou art overtaken by affliction in My path,
> or degradation for My sake, be not thou troubled
> thereby.
> Rely upon God, thy God and the Lord of thy
> fathers.*

Adam quit his job, sold his car, left his house and went to teach the people.

5

He was on the road again. He had nothing but his reliance upon God, a hole in the bottom of each moccasin, and a hand-written sign which said: SOUTH DAKOTA. He soon found that even this was too much. He could not hitch-hike north with a sign having the word SOUTH on it; it confused people. They would stop to tell him that he was going the wrong way. So he threw his sign away and continued north.

A month and a half later Adam was lying on a cot in the cellar of a Bahá'í home on the Rosebud Reservation. A children's class had ended a few hours before and the mid-afternoon heat had put him to sleep soon after it had concluded. He awoke that day to the vibrations of the floating dream; he let them slowly flutter out of him. But left in this world once again he grew sad and reflective. He had accomplished nothing. He had failed as a scholar; he had failed as a laborer; he was now failing as a missionary. Perhaps he should have stayed with God and the goats on the hills in the south of France.

He had come to the Sioux Reservation and joined a Bahá'í Youth

* Bahá'u'lláh, *The Tablet of Aḥmad.*

Project. He taught Bahá'í classes for the Indian children; and he visited the adult Bahá'ís, chatting and telling them a little more about the Faith when the opportunity arose. But Adam did not get along well with other members of the project. He was angry, often quarrelsome, and perpetually silent. Perhaps he didn't feel his talents were being used; but then, he didn't really know what his talents were. Perhaps it was the style that didn't appeal to him: he was not an outgoing, chatty kind of person. But he honestly loved the people he met – he loved their history, their culture and traditions, their simplicity, and the way their faces wrinkled when they grew old; if only he could learn to express his love.

Then two events occurred, each having a profound effect upon him. The first was an unexpected opportunity to live with a Bahá'í family for a short while. This was not a part of the project, but a break from it. He had never before seen so intimately Bahá'í family life; his heart opened to the experience, being swayed by their loving and their listening – to each other and to him. He found this a third fruit of the Revelation of Bahá'u'lláh: having understood the power of the written word, having been made aware of the changes brought about within himself, he was now seeing clearly the changes brought about in the larger world. This family, and the knowledge that there were others like it scattered throughout the world – seed from a sower's hand that a new crop might grow and a new harvest be gathered – gave Adam strength to believe, strength to work.

The second occurrence was the arrival of a girl from Oregon; she had come to join the last month of the project. She came like light into his darkness and like a shining to his dull inabilities. It was not her beauty or her grace or her charm – but surely she was the manifestation of each of these – that changed Adam. It was the radiance of her faith. She believed that things could be done. She believed that she, through the grace of God, could do them. And she believed that Adam could do them too.

In his heart Adam believed these things also, but he had forgotten that he believed them. Deborah reminded him. She was his rescuing angel. During the last month of the summer the two of them worked alone; the others had returned to their homes. Together they served through their combined love for the people they served. Their love accomplished wonders. There was one young Indian whom they met and spoke with one afternoon on the Standing Rock Reservation, who would, perhaps, one day become a Bahá'í and join his strength to that of a world community. He needed to be seen and loved and made aware of the reality of the Cause, but he could never be found. When they went to his home he was not there; when they went to his workplace he was not there. He seemed to have disappeared like the morning mist over the grasslands. Then it happened one day that they were sitting on the grass beside the Catholic Church saying prayers and he suddenly walked toward them from out of nowhere; he said that he had heard their prayers. This happened not once but many times. When they wanted to speak to this man, they did not go to his home or his job site, they went to the grass near the church and said prayers – sooner or later he would appear. In this way he learned about the Faith and Adam learned to have faith.

The summer ended and Deborah and Adam went their separate ways. Deborah had school to attend in Oregon and Adam joined another teaching project in southern California. But they never forgot each other; indeed, it was Deborah who brought out the strength, the resolution and the ability in Adam to continue teaching. Her belief in him caused him to believe in himself and to flower again.

He taught the Faith alone and with others for another four months. As he traveled with other Bahá'ís from border town to border town and migratory camp to migratory camp his joy increased until it knew no bounds. He would arise in the morning with a song in his heart, be challenged all the hours of the day, and fall asleep at night with a prayer upon his lips. His patience and his search had led him to faith and love and hope, these three that endure.

It was as if he had never loved before; soon love would enwrap him entirely. He grew to believe in the hope the future held, and was ready to work that that future might become a reality. He grew to have faith. Faith, that much maligned, much misunderstood and misapplied strength, was, for Adam, the culmination of his search. Faith was knowledge, obedience, a reliance upon God and service in progressive combination. Adam grew to appreciate the words of 'Abdu'l-Bahá to the pilgrims, the words that so often held his heart and moved his lips: 'As your faith is, so shall your powers and blessings be . . .'

'*As your faith is, so shall your powers and blessings be*'

(Thenaud, 'Traité de la cabale'; Bibliothèque de l'Arsenal, Paris. Courtesy of Niedeck Linder, Zurich)

CHAPTER II

*Being how Adam is enraptured by love and how
discordance with love's laws destroys a community
and flings its members to the ends of the earth*

And he (Joseph) lifted up his eyes, and saw his brother Benjamin,
his mother's son, and said, Is this your younger brother, of whom
ye spake unto me? And he said, God be gracious unto thee, my son.
And Joseph made haste; for his bowels did yearn upon his brother:
and he sought where to weep; and he entered into his chamber, and
wept there. And he washed his face, and went out, and refrained
himself.

Genesis 43:29–31

I

The twelfth of November is a day of celebration. It is the
anniversary of the birth of Bahá'u'lláh. It is a day of promise and
hope realized, a day in celebration of faith confirmed, a day of love
and rapture: 'Hark! The herald angels sing / Glory to the new-born
king!' But for Adam, presumptuous though it may sound, it was
more than this, for on this day his soul changed.

He had been teaching the Cause and had grown strong as a
consequence. He had grown courageous, audacious, eloquent, even
wise. But best of all, the song in his heart, stifled so early in life,
began to sound again. It grew slowly at first as he broke the bonds
that held him. It grew stronger and louder until its music broke from
his lips as he walked the autumn streets, and caused the birds, and
the trees, and the very earth, to respond in chorus. His dream and his
prayer were fulfilled.

His heart's song grew to crescendo on the day of celebration.
Then it fell to sudden, desperate silence. It was true he had served, he
had loved; but how could this service be acceptable in the sight of
God? What was love but an ugly hypocrisy when it flowed from a

stained and sullied heart? Did any man reach for the hand of his friend when his own hand was unclean? Did any man approach his bride on her night unwashed and with the odor of drink and another woman about him? No; to do so was more than discourtesy, it was a crime to stain the soul of man. How much greater the crime, how much more impossible, then, to reach to the Friend with a mind stained by sensuality or to approach the Beloved with a heart sullied and impure, smelling of the odor of a stranger? The silence of Adam's heart was desperate and ached for a sound.

What sound could relieve the tension, save one? What sound could release the floodgates but that one which he was not strong enough to utter? But what choice had he? Chastity was the sound upon which all others were scaled. Chastity was more, Adam began to understand, than the mere refraining from physical intimacy – that was but its most blatant realization – chastity was the curbing of desire, the leashing of the mind, and the restraining of the heart. Chastity was not letting oneself be seduced by oneself. Adam had a guilty conscience; guilt trailed him like footprints in the sand. He knew all this: he knew he could not take another step forward without commitment – he knew he was unworthy to love or to receive love – but greater was his knowledge that he could not turn away, that he could not step back.

All that he could think of was the story of the Bahá'ís who had caused Bahá'u'lláh untold suffering and shame because they thought that the murder of three Covenant-breakers would ease the hardship and cease the harassment of an imprisoned community. But of these Bahá'u'lláh had said: 'My captivity cannot harm Me. That which can harm Me is the conduct of those who love Me, who claim to be related to Me . . .'

Adam envisioned his own actions – the glance of his eye, the cast of his thought – as staining the robe of the Beloved, as channeling with tears the face of the Friend. He wept, in his heart and with his eyes, for his own weakness.

On that night, as he sat at a small table away from the music and cried, he wrote to the Universal House of Justice. Anguish was the pen with which he styled his words. He asked for prayers. In his heart he vowed himself to a stronger chastity than he had yet practised. This vow, a vow he would not even be strong enough to keep, was enough: God is less demanding of man than man himself is. Does not the grieved one pray, 'O God! Thou art more friend to me than I am to myself. I dedicate myself to Thee, O Lord.'

It was enough; it was the forward step, the release of tension, the sound that needs be sounded. And it was accepted, for, as suddenly as it had died, his heart's song sprang to life again.

It was, suddenly, as if Adam were encased in a bubble of love – it pressed and filled him, within and without, and on all sides – and was blown, along with unnumbered other bubbles, from a child's plastic soap-bubble pipe. He rose and floated through the air to the sounds of children's laughter and children's music. He was the naked little boy who was taken away into the small world of fairies, who slid down the blades of grass into great, great ponds of dew. Adam had read about that little boy when he was much younger; he had always wanted to read that wonderful story again . . . but now there was no need: he had become the little boy, naked and wrapped in love, and floating in a bubble.

2

Adam turned twenty-one in the middle of December and that simple change, coupled with his desire to serve, made him an administrative asset to the Bahá'í community. He approached the Regional Teaching Committee and told them that he was interested in moving to some small town where he could be of greatest use. They consulted and then told him of two towns not so very far away. One did not yet have an Assembly of nine adults but was growing. The other had a poorly functioning Assembly – having lost some of its most capable members earlier in the year – and it was dying. They suggested he go to the first; he chose the second.

He chose the second because it was an Assembly, because it was in the mountains, it was further from a city, and it was romantically named Good Hope; but most of all he chose it because a woman he had met and taught with during the Fall had also recently moved there. The decision to go to Good Hope was not bad in itself but his motives were not selfless; they were confused, as much fancy as anything else. Fancy is not a strong base on which to build anything. It crumbles soon, and when it crumbles it often takes much good with it. Adam was an incurable romantic – and he did not know this. But he was soon to learn.

The town of Good Hope had eight Bahá'ís residing in it. All were younger than twenty-five and all were unmarried or recently

134

divorced. These eight experimented with the concept of a community. When Adam first arrived there was some rush of excitement. The Local Spiritual Assembly, which had not been meeting, met again; with the transfusion of Adam's energy the Assembly began to pull together, the willful and the weak, and it began to look as if there were yet possibilities in Good Hope. They began to teach and to invite teachers from other Bahá'í localities to come to Good Hope and help them. Excitement was on the rise.

Adam would have had the Assembly meet twice a week but he was reproached for being too headstrong; the Assembly struggled to meet once every two weeks. And at that it was a wonder that anything was accomplished because each meeting was as full of reproaches and recriminations as it was of the possibilities of teaching. Somehow these two widely different aspects merged and got lumped together under one title: survival of the community. Not infrequently someone left the meeting in tears or in a rage. When there are this many young people isolated in a community (that by its very nature must be close knit and closely interacting) with the burden of chastity imposed upon them (in a society that is anything but chaste) there is tension. Every fancied slight or affection, every friendship that might be more, every rivalry – unreal though it be – builds layer upon layer until there is the inevitable outbreak of misplaced and misunderstood emotion. There was nothing stable about this community. It was like some newly-created particle spinning through a physicist's reactor, bombarded and ready to explode. It is not mature and cannot become mature. It cannot last.

Gradually there came to be two factions in the community. There were those who were hopeful and who were teaching and those who were apathetic and would not; those who were excited and those who were bitter. Each faction aggravated the other. It was a mess and growing worse as Riḍván approached. No one was right and everyone was in some degree of frustration and despair.

3

Love is a thing beyond reason, and being beyond reason it knows no bounds. It knows not its own lacking or its own excesses. It will not be made accountable for itself; it is itself and that is sufficient. There are many degrees of love and expressions of love, but all are known by their pain. Where do human and divine love meet and find their expression without conflict? When is compassionate love burning too high and dispassionate love smouldering?

Adam went to Good Hope, his whole being enraptured by love. He went because he wanted to serve, he wanted to offer his love in visible expression; he also went because there was a woman there whom he could grow to love. Mary had taught him, for the brief while that they had been together in the south, about sharing, about a deeper selfless service, about patience. She had left the teacher's strong imprint upon his soul. But why this continued attraction to her? Was it high or lowly? She had seen Adam's potential and had strengthened him by believing in him. Only love sees and brings forth the potential latent in another human being. But what kind of love did this? What more did any man desire than a woman who believed in him? Why did Adam go to Good Hope? He, himself, did not know. He knew only that love had pulled his life from out his hand, as a cyclone will pull a tree out of the ground, and flung him there.

But Mary was, in many ways, not a part of Good Hope at all. She lived there but she arose every morning at five and went to work in the city sixty miles away; she usually did not return until late in the evening. She was there on the weekends to help with the gatherings, to energize the teaching; she chaired the Assembly meetings but she was not stained by them. She came and went through Good Hope like the shadow of an angel. She was a reminder and a hope and a smile. Her love was dispassionate, perhaps even divine. She was a potent force in the community but not a threat to be reckoned with. She never allowed herself to be lowered in the eyes of those who needed her. She and Adam often taught together and broke the Fast together during the month of fasting. But if their love was ever less than divine, it was only so on Adam's part; his mind often tended to fancies.

And to vain imaginings. Another of the Bahá'ís, one of the two women raising children alone, lived but two blocks from him. Her name was Valery. Her son was the reason they first came together – Adam would walk to her house to play with the boy. He needed a man to play with. Valery and Adam would cook dinner together and talk for long hours about the Faith, the boy, about single women raising kids and all manner of things that seemed important. From their togetherness an attraction grew between them. It was the other side of romanticism – not lofty, but lusty. Valery was a lusty woman: she oozed sensuality, sexuality, the way the night oozes wet mystery. This is a kind of love too – in very opposition to the vow that caused love to enwrap Adam – but a kind of love none-the-less.

Of them all, Mary alone understood dispassionate love: the love of the community, the love of each of the individuals who composed it. She was, in a sense, their teacher; but they did not learn their lessons quickly. Adam was worst of all – he confused his loves as poets often do. His lust, his love for an ideal woman, his desire for his God: these he got all in a jumble and soon could not distinguish one from another. His mind became embroiled in confusion; his heart swelled with pain. Every waking moment was a torment and a pain like unto death but without death's promise of release. Every heated word, every silence between Valery and him, pierced him through; every encouragement, every show of faith between Mary and him, melted him like wax in the wick's fire; every word of Revelation, every yearning in the moonlight, drowned him in tears of his own weeping.

After one Assembly meeting he walked slowly away toward his apartment leaving Mary by her car. He walked down the street wet with an evening's rain and shimmering dim in the light of the street lamps; Mary leaned on her car but did not get in, she watched him walk away. She saw his hands in the pocket of his dress coat, the rain that dripped down inside his collar, his shoulders slightly stooped in thought; just before he was out of the range of her voice, she called, 'You're an angel, Adam!'

Her words floated to him and stopped his homeward shuffle. He turned and smiled because she was the real angel. She smiled back, then got into her car and drove away. But Adam was an angel too. He was an angel of fire and snow: an angel who, but for his tears, would be consumed in the fire of his love; who, but for his love, would be drowned in the ocean of his tears. Adam walked on to his apartment but on arriving he only sat on the outer steps. Soon he was drenched to the bone and assured of a fever. Finally he arose to go inside and sleep, though sleep gave him no release. Love refuses all release . . .

Another night he had left Valery's in no happy mood and sought his bed. But there was no relief. At midnight he arose again, dressed and walked into the streets. He walked on and on, his anguished thoughts paced his mind in rhythm with his steps. After a few hours he came to the bridge over the river that flowed to the east of the town. He rested his head on his hands, his elbows on the wall of the bridge. The river was high with the rains in the mountains and tree branches floated swiftly beneath the bridge. He watched the current tear at the river banks like the tearing at his soul, and his tears began to flow again. They rolled between his fingers and over his lips, down his forearms and dropped from his elbows into the river. His tears were carried along to the sea . . .

There was a small park across the road from Adam's apartment complex. It was the home of a bridge and a flock of ducks and two guardian rows of oaks that lined the canal that ran through the park and on through the town. Adam knew the gnarled roots of every tree, the markings of every duck, every step along the canal's embankment. He walked them in dawn's light and in moonlight. Each night he pondered the words: 'This is a bottomless sea which none shall ever fathom.' 'It is the blackest of nights through which none can find his way.'* Each dawn he walked repeating the verse: 'And if he feareth not God, God will make him to fear all things; whereas all things fear him who feareth God.'† His greatest longing was to long forever, to let the pain eat as the eagle ate at the heart of the chained Prometheus. The pain was like wine, the ache like honey to his lips.

Adam often spent his nights sitting quietly in the corner of his front room listening to the waves as they rushed or lapped or crashed against the stone bulwark of the prison and the rock it was built upon. If he listened carefully he was sure that he could count every wave that came against the walls of the prison city of 'Akká.

4

Love is directionless, it is rhythmless – not that it is without direction or rhythm, rather that it is beyond them. It cannot be written of as one writes of a day on the beach. But it is there – on the beach – in the patterns of confusion that the waves weave: in their crash and their running with equal fervor, and both without motive or will. The song says that 'love makes the world go round'; surely it

* Statements attributed to 'Alí íbn Abú Tálib, the son-in-law of Muhammad, and quoted by Bahá'u'lláh in his treatise *The Four Valleys*. Trans. Marzieh Gail.
† Bahá'u'lláh, *The Four Valleys*. Trans. Marzieh Gail.

*'To let the pain eat as the eagle ate at the heart of a
chained Prometheus'*

(Atlas and Prometheus, The Etruscan Museum, Vatican)

keeps the world spinning. It is the universal force: it holds the world together and it tears it apart. The person caught in its fetters is built up, then thrown down, and from his own ruins he is built up anew. He is never let alone. Love will create worlds and then destroy them at a whim. What is not in harmony with the laws of love is thrown to the ends of the earth.

Good Hope was the stage on which Adam confused his loves and mingled the sweetness of their pains. Good Hope, the community, was a part of the play and could not last beyond the curtain's fall because it too was gripped in the laws of love. Good Hope was like the waves that run and roar, that crash and cough at one and the same moment, that build to some great climax and die at once. Good Hope, the people, were doomed to be thrown apart because they could not live in harmony with the laws of love.

These were the people of Good Hope and what became of them:

Valery, harrowingly and deeply, had experienced the forces that fashion youth in American society. She married after having borne her son. She and her husband became Bahá'ís but the marriage wasn't built on anything substantial and so didn't last. She tried to live by Bahá'í morals and standards of conduct but she was consciously uncomfortable and felt out of place. Hers was a flammable personality and it was this when weighed against Adam's essential calm that caused their differences and their final passionate break. Their major point of contention was the political arena of the women's movement. Adam agreed with the principles involved but not with the methods, the actions, and often not even the specific complaints. But he was not a woman and had not experienced the frustration as fully as a woman does: he could not know the thoughts that assail her mind in the bath or before the mirror, alone on the street at night, in public without a man and in public with a man, or alone and raising a child; he did not have the desperate hope in the women's movement that many a woman does. He bluntly labeled most of it as politics and propaganda and wanted nothing to do with that kind of fight. He tried to help Valery; she thought he was trying to make her decisions for her. They were both insulted and angry and they parted in a torrent of hot words and silences. After Adam left Good Hope, Valery did not stay long. She quit her job and went to the university at Berkeley where she could get a teaching degree and then make a more reasonable living, and where there were others – men and women – active in the movement and sympathetic.

Sarah was the other woman in the community who was raising a child alone. She had been married for four or five years and had divorced only a short time before. She was not bitter: she had a measure of independence, a house, a job in the city and the self-confidence that these things bring. She was not unhappy, and, although busy, she made a point of being on a town volleyball team and of engaging herself socially. She was actively adjusting to a new life-style. She had become a Bahá'í some two years before; the Faith held her mind but had not yet enwrapped her heart. A harmonious Bahá'í community was important to her at that stage of her journey; the Bahá'í community was anything but harmonious. The Assembly meetings so troubled her that she soon stopped attending. The Faith she had espoused, though it should have been a support and a joy, was the part of her life most difficult to cope with. And too, among the Bahá'ís of Good Hope, Roger became her closest confidant and this inevitably painted the picture blacker than it was. By May of that year Sarah had sold her house in Good Hope and moved to an apartment in the city to be nearer her job. She had learned from her experience in Good Hope: she was still a Bahá'í, but she did not take an active part in the community life in the city.

Stephanie was the third of the women in the community who had been recently divorced. Adam had known her for many years and while in Good Hope they grew to be close friends. She rarely talked about the divorce though it was still in process, and she followed Bahá'í laws closely and completely in this respect. She expanded her mental and spiritual horizons by concentrated effort. She had begun to build herself a career and was competent and professional in a field where few women venture. Before the Riḍván elections in April, the divorce was finalized and she moved to a new and better job in Idaho. There she faced some real soul-searching upon experiencing firsthand the close and loving atmosphere of the Mormon community. This was especially poignant after the total collapse that was visited upon Good Hope. Though in confusion and doubt for a time, she never lessened her service in the Bahá'í community. It was this that finally eased her mind and soul.

Roger had no capacity to trust. Where there is no open trust, there few other qualities can grow. He was from southern California and his life had been one long, sad, bad experience – he had seen the underside of the great American dragon's belly. It was ugly and it stank; it was no wonder he could not trust. Some years earlier he had undergone a Christian conversion and had worn all the trappings of a fanatic that an American religious convert is likely to wear. But after a while he realized what he had done, began his relationships anew with his family and friends, soon came to hear of the Bahá'í Faith, studied it and joined the community. He still held the Faith somewhat in the light of his Christian experience, as many Bahá'ís did.

Because of his fateful incapacity his career in the Faith had been stormy. He brought the storm with him to Good Hope when he arrived. At first he shared a house with Thom but because both of them were outspoken personalities – Thom honestly and Roger not so much so – they were unable to get along at such close quarters. A person who cannot trust sows distrust so that he may not be alone in the world, and this was the cause of many reproaches and emotional outbreaks in the community. When he moved he moved to the apartment complex where Adam lived and from that day forward the relationship that Adam and Valery had begun to build and work with deteriorated. There was no rivalry, only a horrible distrust of motives and actions. Adam first welcomed him and tried to come to know him, but after perceiving his character, left him to himself. Adam still had a tinge of self-righteousness about him and this did nothing to help matters.

Two important incidents occurred between Adam and Roger which, in Adam's eyes, explained the way things concluded for Roger. One happened the first time Adam entered Roger's apartment. The apartment was no different from his own except that there was no wall between what would have been the bedroom and the living-room. There was only one enlarged sitting-room. On one of the walls hung a poster which immediately captured Adam's eye. It was a full facial photograph of Albert Einstein and a caption which read: 'Great spirits are hindered by little minds.' Adam sat down in a chair and stared hard at the poster. He thought long and hard about the words and finally decided that Einstein would not have written them in a vindictive mood; perhaps in a philosophic mood, but much more likely in a reflective mood and most probably in reference to his own spirit and his own mind. Then Roger said, 'True, isn't it?' with that certain proud expression and intonation that let Adam know immediately that they had understood the meaning of the words in very different ways. Adam did not answer.

The second incident occurred about a month later, around

midnight, and again in Roger's apartment. The two of them were having a heated discussion. The topic roared around to the Faith and to the concept of God. Roger declared that Bahá'u'lláh was God and it was to Him that Bahá'ís prayed. Adam could not accept this because of the manner in which it was conveyed. It was nothing less than the rigidity and paralysis that had afflicted Christianity from its earliest centuries. When the early Christians crushed the heresies, they crippled themselves. Doubtless there were Bahá'ís who had come to believe much of the propaganda disseminated by the charismatic Christian revival and then simply applied it to their own Faith and Founder. Adam had met and worked with Bahá'ís who spoke of a personal relationship with Bahá'u'lláh in much the same way as born-again Christians spoke of Jesus as their personal Savior. This was a more flowing proposal than the one Roger had expressed, but Adam was not particularly fond of it either. Christianity, Adam had decided, was like a dying animal and such things as the charismatic movement were nothing more than the death throes of the stricken creature. They were not things to be mimicked by a young, a live and a thriving religion. What Roger had said was ultimately true, but in a way and in a mystical realm which Roger did not understand and could not reach. On his lips a great truth took on the character of death and falsehood. Adam tried to explain the complexity and inherent dangers of such an opinion but found himself incapable. The expression of love came hard to Adam that night. By May Roger had also left Good Hope, following Sarah to the city. Within a few months he officially resigned from the Faith.

Mary was the light of Good Hope and when she left the sun hid behind the clouds and hope fled. She had been born and raised a Catholic as Adam had been, and she was the youngest and only daughter of a moderately large family. She was a loving and devoted daughter, but when the time came for her to assert her independence she did so vigorously and unsparingly, and she won. Then as ties broke, the relationship with her mother slipped a notch or two also; although they would again be friends, their relationship would never be what it once was. When she went to school so far away in California, however, she found the world an unloving and rainy place – she had 'seen clouds from both sides now'. Her days darkened almost irretrievably until she noticed one light, single and alone, amid the gathering clouds. A friend – more a mere acquaintance really – had not ceased smiling like all the other people. His head was high, and hope and certitude walked abroad when he walked. Mary asked him why he smiled, and he told her about Bahá'u'lláh and the Cause. She wiped away her tears and became a believer. She finished her schooling, taught the Faith in southern California for a summer and a fall, and then went to Good Hope. She was ablaze with light and heat and it radiated from her infectiously. Good Hope basked in her sunshine, everyone grew through her love; but Good Hope was only a stage on her journey. She could not be held by the mud that flowed and settled there. By Riḍván she fulfilled a long-standing dream and went to Sarawak. While she was yet in Good Hope she had taught Adam to smile; her simple command to smile, given on a street corner one afternoon, not only radically changed his appearance and effect, but caused him to love her, perhaps differently from the way he should have.

Thom was the first native of Good Hope to declare his faith in Bahá'u'lláh and he held within him all the promise that that distinction implied. He had been born and raised among the sawmills. His father had worked in them until he died of an unwarranted and unnecessary injury, and then Thom worked in them – he had no choice. He was a creative, intelligent and independent son of the lower middle class trapped by its ethic and its life-style. But he was capable of taking the step that only the few take, and through a carefully cultivated love and guidance he became a Bahá'í. As a Bahá'í he flowered. He grew audacious in his questioning and strong and independent in his ability to think situations through and discover the truths hidden deep within them. He was no longer afraid or bound. Adam had first met him when he took the initiative and drove to South Dakota to teach children's classes on the reservations for a month. Adam, who had always traveled, did not realize at the time what a show of strength that act was. But he knew he liked Thom, and, though their opinions frequently clashed, he knew he would always like him. Thom had come into the Faith through the love of some of the early Bahá'ís in Good Hope, but when they left the community began to crumble and he was somewhat at a loss what to do and how to help. He offered what he could – chiefly his undeviating and unconditioned honesty – and stood back and watched. Somehow he took it all in stride and was not wounded; he had grown strong of his own initiative by then. He took up painting again after having left it when he left school. He was obviously talented, but the most fascinating thing about his painting was that it measured and reflected the tensions, frustrations and joys of the community life in Good Hope. Some of the canvases bore ominous clouds on the horizon and dreary mill town scenes with workmen, dusty and with dour faces, returning to their homes in the reddish-gray dawn. Others bore lighter, more hopeful, mountain landscapes or seascapes. One painting was a singularly beautiful yellow rose, without a background other than an incomplete light gray wash. The yellow rose was suspended in the center of the canvas and the single word 'Sarah' was roughly etched in the lower right-hand corner. There was no signature. He gave it to Sarah when she was feeling ill one week. Thom and Adam left Good Hope together in late April and went to South Carolina to join a teaching project. They taught the Faith together and apart for almost three months before Thom felt the itch to move on again. He and a few others went to the Louisiana oilfields to look for work. Thom took his paints with him when he went.

By the early summer following that Riḍván no one remained in Good Hope except Marcie. Marcie was a child in a crippled woman's body who was satisfied as a child is and was taken care of as a child needs to be. She knew nothing of the Faith to which she belonged except the love that was sprinkled upon her throughout the storms. When summer came she only knew that those who had come to see her and bring her chocolates no longer came. She cried. Then she stopped crying because her world was sad and one more sadness was not noticed for long.

These, then, are the characters who play at love's game and cross love's stage. Love finds each one worthy or unworthy by its own measure and not by any measure we can take. It brings these players together to dance for a bit and then flings them apart each unto their own destiny. Love cares for its players not at all, for when the dance is over it throws down the curtain and even the stage is no more.

CHAPTER III

*Being how love succeeds and how it succeeds not;
also being why Adam is compelled to leave his
homeland*

Then Joseph could not refrain himself before all them that stood by him; and he cried, Cause every man to go out from me. And there stood no man with him, while Joseph made himself known unto his brethren. And he wept aloud: and the Egyptians and the house of Pharaoh heard. And Joseph said unto his brethren, I am Joseph; doeth my father yet live? And his brethren could not answer him; for they were troubled at his presence. And Joseph said unto his brethren, Come near to me, I pray you. And they came near. And he said, I am Joseph your brother, whom ye sold into Egypt. Now therefore be not grieved, nor angry with yourselves, that ye sold me hither: . . . God sent me before you to preserve you a posterity in the earth, and to save your lives by a great deliverance. So now it was not you that sent me hither, but God.

Genesis 45:1–8

I

When coarse, black coal – the dross of the earth – is stolen out of the ground, attacked, beaten and broken, thrown into the fire, burned by slow degrees until its pain and torment rise like smoke on the wind, the forces which cause this seem untouched by the suffering; they might be said to play with the ugly, black dross like an unfeeling child plays with some small insect until it dies. But this black flower, this gem from beneath the clay, laughs and rejoices in the end. It succeeds through the forces that torment it. It reveals its true reality by casting away its dull, black outer garment and donning the attributes of the fire. It becomes heat and light itself. From the earthly, it becomes celestial. So it is too when men are mined from out the rut of their predictable world and thrown into love's fire. So it was with Adam when he was uprooted and cast into Good Hope. In that place he was burned and beaten until he became the very attribute of the love that treated him so. Love confirmed him and he slipped from out its grasp as a drop of love itself.

Sometimes, at night, Thom and Adam walked together and talked. Some nights they walked the streets of Good Hope and some nights they drove into the mountains and walked the lumber companies' roads. These walks were not always easy – their strides were different. When Thom walked, he ran; when Adam walked, he crawled. Maybe it was that Thom wanted to see everything while Adam wanted to miss nothing. But with only mild irritations they adjusted to each other's pace and, although it was infrequent that they walked shoulder-to-shoulder, it was also infrequent that they were not in speaking range. One such evening, as they walked past a stand of pine that had been felled but not yet dragged away, Adam called out to Thom's disappearing figure, 'Slow down, there's no need to take life so fast. Pretty soon you'll be like that little girl in the market today: turned on her mother's shoulder to see what she missed.'

Thom stopped and waited for Adam to mosey on up. Then he said, 'You're strange. You know that?'

'Yeh?' and he flashed a smile. This was going to be good: either an extended reprimand – which, because Thom was forthright but never malicious, would not hurt too much – or a fortune-telling session – and Adam had always taken a secret delight in having his fortune told.

Thom was undaunted by the 'Yeh?' and launched into his point.

'There is something strange about you and it's hard to make out exactly what. You don't dress like anybody I ever met and you haven't any distinguishable accent. Maybe all your moving about has done something to you!' Adam exhaled a half-chuckle and Thom went on, 'But not only that, there's also something about the way you act that doesn't quite set right. Like you're acting or you're not really showing who you are. There's a slight whiff of hypocrisy about the things you do.'

'Like how?'

'Well, if it's not hypocrisy, it's something like it. It's hard to place you; to know what you really mean. Or who you really are.' Then reflectively, 'But maybe only God knows who anybody really is.'

He paused for a few seconds and Adam picked up, 'Give me an example.'

'Maybe it's not hypocrisy. Maybe it's self-righteousness or something. Well, like your telling Roger that he shouldn't play the bingo and sweepstakes tickets that they give away in the supermarkets. You told him it was putting his hopes on games of chance. Bad chance, I think you emphasized. You said that Bahá'u'lláh enjoined us to put faith in God, not chance and fortune. You even compared it to gambling. That's a stretch of the imagination, you gotta admit. But even if all you said was true and, who knows, maybe it was, even so, you shouldn't have said it.'

'Why not?'

'Lots of reasons why not. For one, it's just plain none of your business whether he picks up and plays those stupid little tickets or not. Not unless he asks you. And for another, even if he had asked you, he still wasn't ready to hear that. All you did was make him play those games more stubbornly. You want me to go on?'

'No, no. I get the point. You're right, I've got to work on that. I lost a good friend once because of self-righteousness. But it's a hard thing to distinguish from righteousness and not easy to get out of the system. But how 'bout hypocrisy?'

'I don't know. Just something . . . Do you know what "evanescent" means?'

'Yeh.'

'I thought maybe you didn't. It's in the Long Obligatory Prayer. I only looked it up a few days ago.'

'I had to look it up a while back myself.' He paused. 'You know, I've thought about this a lot. Hypocrisy, even though it's so severely denounced, is still a relative thing. For example, when you read in your book of modern American painters and you find someone or something you like, you begin to use it in your own painting. You copy it, trying to make it a part of your style even though it's not you. You put it on and off like you would a coat until it either fits or you discard it. That's the way the old apprentice system worked, more or less. When you copy a master and your motive is to learn and grow, then the imitation, though it is not yet you, will never be hypocrisy.

'It's the same with spiritual and moral growth. We usually acquire virtues by imitation. As Bahá'ís we have a Master and Exemplar who calls us, saying, "Look at Me. Follow Me. Be as I am", and it is our challenge and privilege to try to do just that. We try to make His virtues our own by wearing them until they fit —

until we've grown into them. Usually the fit isn't right at first: the garment is ungainly and the character is uneven. That's not because we're untrue to ourselves; but because our selves are changing. We are becoming our true selves.'

'Makes sense, I guess. Did you tell me once that you were in England as a kid?'

'Yeh; for three years, but I was real young. I don't remember a thing about it – not that that means much, I don't remember what I had for breakfast this morning either. Why?'

'Maybe that explains it.'

'Explains what?'

'Explains why you're not easily understandable. Why there's that little bit of mystery about you. You're not really an American. You're something different.'

Adam laughed. 'Well, maybe. Sometimes I don't feel very American.'

'You don't suppose . . . Say, let me see your left hand.' Adam gave him his hand. 'No. The other one, dummy. Didn't you ever learn your left from your right?'

'I guess I had a deprived childhood.'

'Well, the little finger's straight. At least you're not a Martian.'

'Say, I've applied to work at the House of Worship in Wilmette this summer; but I'm beginning to feel like leaving after Riḍván if we can't pull an Assembly off. There's a teaching program in South Carolina. Would you be interested in going?'

'Be specific. Going where; when?'

'Going . . . slow down, will you . . . going to the National Convention in Wilmette at the end of April and then going to South Carolina for the month of May.'

'I'm working, remember?'

'So am I. So what. Take a month's vacation; or better yet, give the company notice and quit. You don't like the work anyway.'

'Sometimes the things you say really irk me. They usually have all kinds of hidden propositions in them.'

'Now what?'

'I can't just up and quit my job even if I don't particularly like it. I've risen some in the company and I've got some benefits because my dad worked there too. If I quit I lose all that. Good jobs aren't easy to come by, you know. And if I found another job, it'd probably be at three dollars an hour less than I'm making now. May happens to be the beginning of the heavy summer season too. These mountains are beginning to dry by then and they can get the heavy equipment up here again. It's doubtful if they'd give me a month's vacation then.'

'Well, if you don't ask you won't get anything.'

Thom was still hot about the subject, 'All this traveling of yours and your romantic plans to visit the Temple in Panama simply because there's a road that goes all the way there! There's also a war in Nicaragua in case you hadn't heard. If you'd buy a radio at least you'd know what's happening in the world. It's made you irresponsible. You've never held a job for more than a year. You just get up and go somewhere. You've never felt trapped in a job. You say: give the company notice and quit. Well, fine. But you say it too easily.'

'Wait a minute, now. I've felt trapped before too. Maybe not by a job, but by other things. And the oppression of being trapped is just as heavy, no matter what traps you.'

'We've been out teaching together and I've listened to you talk to some of these working men about the Faith. After a bit they ask you where you're from (because they know you're not from here). Usually you answer, with your secret pride, that you're "from all over" or "from many places". The muscles on their faces tighten at that, my friend. Every time. Maybe, if you're not too involved with what you're speaking about, you'll add that your old man was in the Air Force and you had to move a lot as a kid. That helps to moderate the effect on these people, at least to some extent. But believe me, you lose half your audiences because they ask where you're from. Suddenly, you might just as well be a hippy in their eyes. And they don't think much of hippies, at all! They think they're irresponsible and even disloyal. They know that you don't know what it's like to be trapped.'

'I'll watch myself more carefully. All the same, it's just too easy to say I've never been trapped and don't know what it's like. You told me that you'd been trapping in these woods with your father when you were younger. And you told me that there were two kinds of animals that got caught in your steel traps. There was the beaver or muskrat that would get a foot in the trap and spring it. It'd be caught and after some struggle it would just lie down and die. If the trap had got it, it'd be there and you'd have the pelt. But then, there was the other kind of animal – like the silver fox – and it would never be in a sprung trap. A paw might still be there, but the animal itself was gone. It valued its freedom so much that it'd chew off its own paw. Even if it just went away and died somewhere, it wouldn't be in that trap! It wouldn't die in the trap. It's the same with people: some die in the trap and some refuse to, but that doesn't mean that they've never known the trap with all its steel teeth. Most people are like the muskrat, but I'm like the fox. If there weren't a few three-legged foxes around, there wouldn't be any muskrat either – they'd have given up long ago and trooped into the traps to die.'

'I'll think about asking for a month's leave. There's the truck; let's head back. I have to work the morning shift tomorrow. I've never seen anybody walk as slow as you.'

Three weeks later they were in Thom's pickup heading towards South Carolina. Good Hope had splattered like a raw egg dropped on the floor, and everyone was gone or going soon. They had gambled and lost.

Thom had asked for a month's leave and, as he had thought, it was denied. He got angry and he quit. Adam had had second thoughts about his ever suggesting such a drastic action in the first place, but Thom enjoyed the episode enormously. He even took a week before they left and devoted it entirely to painting. The back of Thom's pickup was packed with his painting equipment, his stereo and his clothes. There was just enough room for a mattress down the centre of the truck's bed. Thom had begun to talk of staying in the southeast for a while even though he hadn't seen it yet. The stereo, to which Thom was singularly attached, was the greatest proof that he might do just that. He was capable of it.

When they crossed the South Carolina state line Thom had a few thousand dollars in his pocket. Adam had six dollars and eighty-three cents. They had been splitting the costs of gas and oil evenly and Adam had figured his budget almost to the penny.

2

That's when they met Myriam. Myriam was one of those unique individuals who totally upset the New York City machine and get spit out of Brooklyn from time to time. She was part nineteen-sixties rebel and part Peter Pan. She must have been about thirty-five, but there was no way to tell: she was ageless. With a thick, Jewish, New York accent, a short punchy body, flaming red hair quickly brushed back to her shoulders but in her eyes again an hour later, and always in jeans and a loose cotton shirt that she must have confiscated from her husband when he stopped hunting and began going to Wall Street, Myriam was the kind of fiercely independent woman about whom the establishment always wondered and after whom it was always casting second glances. Every establishment! She just wasn't classifiable by any standard. But she was deeply interested in people and uncommonly understanding of the human condition. She could spend hours peeling potatoes for a potato salad to be eaten at the wedding of the brother of a friend's sister-in-law knowing full well that she couldn't go to the wedding or even be invited because she would be the only white 'people' there. And that would cause more problems than anybody wanted to handle. She would talk and laugh about the absurd conventions that prejudice had spawned, all through the peeling session. Her laughter, echoed by the other ladies peeling potatoes, would ring through the house and spill out into the street of some little backwoods community where everyone knew her and loved her. When she would have to leave, late in the afternoon or early in the evening, to go back to the city and pick up her children and feed them, half the population of the little house-trailer and concrete block encampment would turn out to push her car until it coughed itself to life, and wave goodbye to her through the thick dust raised on the unpaved road.

Being with Myriam was to experience the pageant of human life. Each day was full – full from six in the morning until midnight: full with bouncing children; full with the veteran who had given his leg and his marriage for his country and who had nothing now but his bitter resentment against the country that had taken them; full with the three sisters, ages fourteen, seventeen, and nineteen – the older two with babies still crawling – who kept their shotgun loaded to frighten away the rats and men who, come nightfall, came slipping through the holes in the walls of the half-collapsed shack they called their home; full of talk and problems, undiminished hope dispensed day after day after day, and, on occasion, filmstrips whose theme was racial amity and world unity; full of potato peeling and pea poddings; full with attending the funeral of a young girl with whom you had been talking and laughing only last week, then, later in the day, visiting a VISTA-organized children's kindergarten taught by another young girl with whom you had also been just last week; full with a hundred miles every day in a car that might get you where you were going but could not be counted on to get you back again; full of isolated roads that weave their way between the swamps and bogs and woods to the hundred little townships each consisting of a dozen houses, a small factory, and maybe a general store and a post office settled on the intersection, with another isolated, meandering road going nowhere in particular, or to an actual town (with churches and stores and a main street) where there might be two Bahá'ís or no Bahá'ís at all because only the white people actually lived within the town limits – the other 'town' began at the city limits sign: it was busting at its seams with running children, old men smoking pipes on porches, women hoeing gardens, people falling off rooftops because they had climbed them when they were stumbling drunk and had just woken up to find themselves with a blinding hangover and no ladder, it was bursting with laughter, excitement, frustration, fear and joy, it was alive – unlike the town itself which had died, been preserved and was lying in state waiting for some official function – it was where a hundred black Bahá'ís lived. This was where the roads went, what the days were full of, and what it was like for Thom and Adam to be teaching with Myriam.

Teaching the Faith with Myriam was an exciting, joyous experience; that could never be doubted. Every day there were new insights, new growth, and new, small developments and advances. But it was the slow, building excitement of raising and educating a child and patiently awaiting the fruits of maturity. Or it was like planting and tending young fruit trees. There was noticeable growth at a constant rate but still it took years before the trees would be fruit-bearing. It was the total change and real growth implied in the transformation of consciousness; but for young, anxious teachers like Thom and Adam it seemed a long, slow fuse on a great keg of dynamite. They wanted fireworks. They can't be blamed. When this was realized, explained, and consulted about, the outcome was to design an intensive three-day study course (a baptism in the stream of Bahá'u'lláh's writings). Then, more than merely wet behind the ears, they could try to make their own explosion.

The course, given to a small group of six or seven, was itself an explosion: an explosion of awareness that occurs only rarely in a person's life, a time when barriers, previously unrecognized, are suddenly revealed, then thrown down and wide, ever-widening horizons are realized on every side. Adam had known for many years that heaven and hell were states of his own creating that existed at every stage of life, but suddenly it was as if this knowledge was clearly manifested and heaven was a dramatic daily experience that could be attained and held. He knew 'the bliss of mystic knowers' as a silent music enwrapped him. A quiet, serene joy wafted from the lilac and honeysuckle and permeated all the world. There was the certitude that the path was still before him and the goal had drifted even more remotely into the all-encompassing present. It was to touch, once again, his own reality, to realize that the exalted and exalting words uttered by the Godhead were addressed to him, to realize that it was within him to arise and set a continent aflame. Love was confirmed by the experience of knowledge. It was as though for the first time Adam's heart and mind were truly coupled and thereby jointly released into the world of being. His soul had changed.

If the rural people of the southeastern states were the material set for combustion and their open- and pure-heartedness was the fuse, then the enthusiasm and loving excitement kindled in the hearts of Adam and those like him was the spark that could set the region aflame.

Again he went out to meet the people: to talk, to teach, to serve, and to share the secret of joy. Though no two days were alike, patterns developed: personal patterns, patterns in communities, patterns in teaching, and patterns of acceptance. Adam would rise at dawn, shower and go out to a small stand of elm and pine where someone had quietly buried a handful of dust from the place of Quddus's martyrdom. There in the peace and pleasing warmth of the rising sun he offered his daily prayers. Sometimes he knew his prayers were accepted by the way that the early morning light shimmered on the leaves that fluttered in the breeze; sometimes he knew by the mosquitoes that came to tell him to take no notice of them, that Zoroaster and 'Alí had both been assassinated while deep in prayer; and, on at least one occasion, he knew by the sudden downpour that melted him into the mud and caused him to flow far away into the sea.

After the morning prayers and the division and assigning of tasks they set out in small groups of two or three to find the Bahá'ís and their families. Often they followed an ill-drawn and confusing map or the instructions of people they met on the road and finally they would arrive at a broken-down board shack. As they drove up – as often as not, two men and both as white as nature drew them (they might forget their pale complexions but any observer would know at once how out of place they looked in that neck of the woods) – the children were rushed inside or around back, and a big, really big, Mama would make her stand on the porch. Her feet were set apart and firmly planted, her arms were crossed on her imposing chest, her face was stern and set, her eyes distrustful; there would be fat and muscle and unrelieved tension bulging out everywhere. As they walked up, the first words out of Adam's mouth were an assurance that they were not police or insurance salesmen.

Then muscles relaxed and the stance became less rigid – occasionally they heard the distinct sounds of a shotgun being unloaded and put away inside the house – and the eyes turned from distrust to questioning. As they walked onto the porch Adam said, 'We are Bahá'ís. Are you Mrs. ————?' and the woman's face would light like a neon sign at dusk and she would smile with all the jowl and muscle that had been terrible only a moment before. She would open her arms wide and hug both these strange white boys who were now transformed into long lost and wayward sons returned to the waiting Mama.

Amidst giggles and snickers and blushing, all the children – never less than a dozen of them – were marched out, lined up and inspected for bright eyes, the capacity to giggle uncontrollably if they were tickled and their loud and brash obedience to Mama. If some one of the children was too shy to meet the strangers (and it wasn't an acknowledged case of tender-heartedness) then a pot or a ladle was let fly to show how capable the child was of quickly dodging identified flying objects.

They were ushered inside to sit on the sofa or bed or to huddle near the pot-belly stove if it were cold and raining. Sometimes chairs were brought out onto the porch and everyone sat there and talked. There were long agreements about Jesus and about the basics of the Faith and there were often many confused ideas that would not become clear quickly – probably not in this generation. These people were Bahá'ís, that was sure; but they were also ardent Christians; they called themselves Baptist-Bahá'ís or Holiness-Bahá'ís or whatever the name of the denomination of the church that happened to be nearby. This was not the cause of any disunity, but the sign of a changing awareness, of a biologically-slow, growing consciousness.

Often a spontaneous lesson was given to the children. It was a morals lesson made graphic by a story taken from the over-flowing reservoir of Bahá'í history. Just as often, one of the children, having reached the age of maturity, was pushed forward with the words, 'There's James Jr. here; he's seventeen now. You tell him all about Bahá'u'lláh and see what he says.' Sometimes James Jr. would become a Bahá'í and sometimes not. But never if he didn't want to. Often other family members – uncles, cousins, grandmothers – and all the curious neighbors would swell and build the black waves of humanity gathered about an insignificant white sail on the porch to hear about the Faith, or to pray, or just to talk and laugh. It was good for black and white to laugh together, they said.

Once, Adam remembers vividly, sadness turned into rolling, belly-gripping laughter. That was the nature of these people: nothing could keep them down. In one small back-road conglomeration of houses there had lived a very old man – he was said to have been one hundred and four; he was an upstanding man, wise, loving, kind to a fault; he had been a Bahá'í for twenty years, was outspoken and frequently traveled to nearby towns to teach the Faith. Everyone loved him and turned to him for guidance in all manner of problems. No one expected him to die. But that is what he did. Somehow the Bahá'ís had been told and had attended the funeral. This was their next visit to the community after the death of the old man; it was two months later.

A small mountain of people were sitting on and around a central porch talking about the Faith and saying prayers. There were, amidst this mountain, two very bald, very old men – younger brothers of the man who had died. There were also a flock of half-interested children milling around. Then someone said that a prayer should be read for the old man who had died. It was decided that the eldest of the surviving brothers should say the prayer and that it should be a teaching prayer so that the old man's soul would still keep on teaching everybody even after he had died. Adam gave the brother his prayer book while the brother found his spectacles and adjusted them on his nose. Meanwhile, everyone else had arranged themselves into the most respectable position they could manage. The children were quieted.

The old man began to read the first prayer listed under the section labeled: teaching. He read in a very slow, halting voice but with as much dignity and understanding as he could muster. He had probably not been asked to read aloud for years. He read until he finished a verse which said: '. . . and the hair of my head declareth the power of Thy sovereignty and might. . .' There he stopped for a few seconds and, as he thought about that, unconsciously swept a hand over his bald pate. His brother, just as bald, snickered under his breath and was given a cold eye by one of his daughters. But as the prayer continued a stifled snicker went through the assemblage as one after another realized what had happened. Some could not control their mirth no matter how hard they tried, and the children giggled openly for no other reason than that they had been quiet too long already. Finally the old man, still struggling with the prayer amidst the suppressed outbreaks, came to a passage that read: '. . . and assist me, by Thy strengthening grace, so to teach Thy Cause that the dead may speed out of their sepulchers. . .' and with that the joy and laughter would no longer be contained. Bellies jiggled; men complained that their sides hurt with laughing so hard. The prayer was never finished, but it didn't matter because God loves laughter best of all.

This was the love that succeeds: divine, universal love, unconstrained by the passions that afflict flesh and blood; the love of a new community, of a new future that can be, of a world family bound by just such a love. Adam became a lover of love itself.

When he first arrived in South Carolina he had the good fortune to find the company of a master teacher. Six months later, after a personal conversion and a series of ascending stages and cycles, he grew to be a fine teacher in his own right. When he left South Carolina he did so because of love. Having understood this much, he gambled that other ways of love would be open to him also. They weren't.

3

In South Carolina love was like the air we breathe; it pervaded everything. But Adam began to feel like the Ancient Mariner in the Sargasso Sea when he cried: 'Water, water everywhere / Nor any drop to drink.'

He seldom spoke of Mary. If he mentioned her, she was 'the woman who taught me to smile' or 'the reason why I smile'.

Eventually, however, I was able to see his old letters (or, at least the ones he copied and kept; there were some very obvious holes in the sequence). From these, letters to other friends, and the few stories which he has told me of that year in California, I have been able to piece together the following events.

He had received a few letters from Mary, now far away in Sarawak, and they flowed with that same pervasive love which she showered on everyone. Adam longed for the love to be personal and so at the end of one of his letters, unrelated to anything written above, he asked: Do you want to get married? There was no reason why she should say yes but love is not impeded by mere reason. There was no hope either. This was confirmed each day that an answer did not arrive. But beyond hope there is a certain perseverance that is a distant cousin of assurance, of certitude. Adam anxiously waited on that perseverance until Mary's letter came. It appeared one day in somebody's hand, just appeared as Adam knew it would. This is what it said:

> Alláh'u'Abhá
> Ma_sh_iyyat
>
> Accept this seashell,
> O precious servant
>   to the
> Most Great Ocean,
> as a symbol of
> our future marriage.
>
> It is
> and it will be
> a shelter from storms,
> heat and predators.
>
> Its beauty,
> designed by the
> Wronged One of the World,
> will be a
> solace to the weary soul.

Confirm us,
O Day-Star of the Universe,
with a ray of your brilliance,
that together we may become
lower than the dust
vibrating in devotion to
Thy Most Great Name.

Guide us,
O Most Great Light,
along paths of humble service;
to the heights of detachment
from all but Thee,
O Preserved Treasure;
to peaks radiant with the
light of faith in Thee
O Lord of the Covenant.

Mary

Adam floated on air for three days. He was of absolutely no use to anyone, and on two occasions he had to be told, 'Stop dancing: this is a restaurant!'

He waxed poetic when he wrote back. He released the floodgates of his heart and channeled the streams stored up there. His letters were intense and his verse poor; they were like most letters written by young lovers: the kind that make a person wince if he happens to stumble upon them later. He didn't keep them. Later, when the worst was over, and Adam and Mary had a chance to sit down together and talk, he learned that she had thought his letters insincere. He was deeply hurt by that. Adam was a fool; and being a fool, he was many things, but one thing he was not was insincere. Fools are never insincere.

He wrote that he was leaving South Carolina and returning to California to speak to his parents about the marriage. When he arrived in Eureka there were two letters from Mary waiting for him. He read them in order of their post dates. The first was a hesitation about her answer; the second was a full about-face.

Adam,
It was a few weeks ago – I was getting to know my students. My mood was getting darker and it was hard to find the inner strength to

go to class – then my body started to get weak – then I was sick. You know about heart feelings that say 'do this' and you know it's right and you do it. Well my heart and body said, 'Go and find someone to take care of you now!' so I went over to a Bahá'í's house as she was about to go work – got in the car – her husband (a Bahá'í) took me where I asked to a theological college – the Eisenwald family, I knew, would give me the help I needed. I said to Mrs Eisenwald, 'I need someone to take care of me.'

The food (I was sick, we think, because of undernourishment), the loving family, the bed, the comforts of an American home, made me so happy and thankful to God. I knew this feeling of happiness is what the Master meant when He said, 'Be happy'. I was meant to be happy. This experience made me see that the basic and practical things of life are the important things, they can bring me to God. How right it is to be happy – how basic and simple.

Adam, it was wrong of me to tell you 'yes, I'll marry you'. I should have been more practical and wise. I left you as a friend, meaning that my heart feels the same warmth towards you as toward other Bahá'ís I know. Why did I say 'yes'? Not because my heart said, but because my mind said – 'he is a good, active Bahá'í and he would be good for you and for Sarawak'. I prayed and listened, as the Guardian teaches, for six days – with no definite answer. I only felt the *conviction* that the *Faith is all that matters*. When I got sick (this happened after I sent you my consent) I realized that happiness is a vital part of my FAITH. I haven't yet learned how to have that happiness. Conviction isn't enough to be a good Bahá'í.

I will cause you pain, suffering, and grief now because of my mistake. I should not have said 'yes' when I knew my heart was silent. It was a serious 'yes' of conviction, of serious dedication to the Faith, not a 'yes' out of happiness. I should have told you my heart was neutral – I cannot give you an answer – but felt the answer had to be 'yes' or 'no' – and I thought, I want a companion in my loneliness; he's a good Bahá'í; we're compatible. Do you see how dry these are – compared to 'O God, I'm so happy I could burst. I want to sing and dance with joy. I want to follow him anywhere, do anything, just so I'm with him.' This is how I should feel before I go and tell a man 'yes'. I had no right to consent because my heart is silent concerning you.

If I married you with my heart neutral, oh you know that would cause you such pain and me too. It was a grievous error to tell you 'yes', but better to tell you now.

Your letter came – it helped me make up my mind. Reading about your happiness and joy just magnified my lack of happiness and joy. I remember my ecstasy at being asked to pioneer by the International Goals Committee. *It was right* – my heart and mind were united and the result was great happiness. And here I am – it's hard here but I won't back out because I entered into the agreement with positive one-hundred-percent assurance.

If we were married without one-hundred-percent assurance and happiness – full-brimming like yours is – oh how painful it would be for both of us.

My poor Adam – life gives us such suffering – especially for kinds like you who feel things deeply – you just learned about love and the joy it can bring, you loved me and now I must tell you, my heart does not share the same with your heart. Please continue to love – but I cannot marry you because I know you love me – that would not be sincere.

I am lonely. I want someone to lean on – I need a strong Bahá'í to refresh me when I'm down – you could do these things. But I have to have that happiness and joy, for that is what will attract people. 'Be happy,' says the Master. 'It's hard in a world of suffering', 'It's hard when we don't know how', we say. Bahá'u'lláh says, 'Know yourself to know God.'

I must accept the fact that I'll continue on alone. If I was supposed to have married you God would have revealed to my heart, love. This has not happened – so we must accept – there is nothing else to be done. You must give up your beautiful dreams – please do not stop loving and being happy. God will give you a wife who is crazy in love with you – who will want nothing but the pleasure of standing with you through all sufferings and joy – with you and no-one but you. That is what you deserve. You deserve better than me, for I would be a half-hearted wife – luke-warm – not right.

Adam, I am hurting your tender heart by this letter but please know that I can't help it – I have to accept my feelings; I cannot tell my heart to feel love – it will not obey me. I am sorry.

with Bahá'í love but not marriage love, Mary

P.S. – I am enclosing the unsent letter I wrote before I wrote you the *yes* poem. It says that from the beginning my heart felt no happy love and joy and assurance – it was silent – do you accept that I want to marry with a heart full of love and joy – it is not, so I will not marry.

My dear Adam, Alláh'u'Abhá.

Since your letter arrived Sunday I have thought and prayed every free moment. It would be special for both of us for me to say yes, I will marry you, and most often this week I've felt I could say that except for some points:

1) I must walk my spiritual path with practical feet.

2) I have been assigned a pioneer post, which, the Guardian says, should not be left except for extreme reasons.

Would you be willing to live your earthly life in Sarawak?

3) *Fortress for Well-Being* says I should consider by what means you can support a family – this is harsh-sounding to your tender heart open to me.

4) I respect your virtues and am proud of your ever striving to be a better Bahá'í. My love for you is as one devoted Bahá'í to another devoted Bahá'í. My predicament is – is that all that's needed? Or should there also be a head-over-heels love? Then I ask myself – am I the type to fall head-over-heels; and I ask myself – is that an old American notion?

I haven't felt lonely in Sarawak until this week considering how I'd be if I said no.

I am not prepared to give a yes, no, or maybe answer – because I don't know how I'm supposed to feel.

As a Bahá'í I know the Bahá'í situation here and I know you could help me immensely. What I mean is, if I think of myself as a tool of service to Bahá'u'lláh then I say yes, marrying you would help me learn more virtues, teach the Faith here more, stay here longer, keep my sense of emotional well-being. <u>Khánum</u> says a devoted Bahá'í should marry a devoted Bahá'í. You are a devoted Bahá'í.

We share a child's heart, we share a love of words and books, we share a willingness to live a life without some luxuries, I can speak with you very easily – whereas with many men I cannot.

All these words, Adam! I apologize for my stumbling around in a dark forest – the new growth is entangled by the old. If my spirit were more in control I could give you a clearer answer. I decide yes and what do I feel? not happiness, but grim determination.

Adam, this feeling of grim determination could well be because I know how hard it will be, I mean I have a hint of the difficulties that lie ahead for me as a pioneer in Sarawak – for all of us (people) – the world over – life is very ominous these years of the great purging – Adam, I am comfortable with the thought of sharing that suffering with you, for you and I would help each other keep our faces turned to Bahá'u'lláh. (I know what is important, I will marry him.) (Knowing this world is growing darker by the minute, there is no more time.)

Is that enough for you? To have a wife that feels the above – a wife who would die for you but is not head-over-heels in love. I honestly do not know the answer.

For nine months the battle raged. His letters were intense and romantic; hers were loving and considerate. Each was aggravating to the other. Adam suffered all the pains of love again, and exalted in every terrible moment of it. A friend of his wrote that he brought it all on himself; and his friend was right. Love's pains are self-inflicted; were they not, the lover would not tolerate them, let alone yearn for them as he does.

But the pain was futile save for the knowledge it gave and the movement it caused, for Adam was unlucky in love. The proof was in the palm of his hand.

Adam, Alláh'u'Abhá.

Please continue to write to me! And forget about any pressure – it doesn't exist on this end. What I need now is friendship; don't we all.

I am glad to hear of your special friendship; your understanding of love will deepen even more till you'll be the lover of California – not as beautiful as I was hoping but anyway. I remember how love dawned on your heart and your face reflected its rays – oh your smiling face is a treasure to anyone who partakes.

Oh Adam, your talk of our new believers in Crescent Beach, 'Am I not your lord?' 'Yes, verily', brought a tearful response from my heart. Dear Adam, in our love for our Faith – ours in simple unity – in our love for our Faith we shall always be lovers in our mutual longing to sacrifice ourselves to a flame that, by the wisdom of God, has not yet come to us – the flame of sacrifice and suffering.

Your path, dear dear pure-hearted one – your path may be a path of riches – how well I know you have prepared in yourself a life of renunciation, and how attractive this is. I love you, Adam.

You may possibly prefer the lifestyle of a mystic, a hermit – if our Faith condoned it? – But we are all on this earth to attract people – and most of the people – can they relate to the path of a mystic?

The people here still remember with love the Bahá'í surfer who came here for a year – she had fun fishing and surfing and playing and they loved her. The trick in attraction is happiness and oh you're a magnet when you shine with your smile. Smile, as a gift to me. Adam, I need your letters of love. Please continue to write. I'm lonely. No one here tells me they notice I'm trying to be a good Bahá'í – all I long to share is the Faith – and in your longing for a companion, and mine too, let us continue to console each other with love letters; letters to raise our spirits so we feel invincible, we are joyful as we shout, 'Yes, verily You are our Lord.'

I too long to reach the heights of the love of God – to burn in the love of God, to smile joyfully no matter what hardship assails me. God willing He will carry us both ever forward toward our goals. If you are finished with *Hound of Heaven* – yes, please return it. Just for memories sake, what else do you have of mine? I have your picture of the Master and your *Bahá'í World Faith* – I treasure both – I love you, Adam, and I am happy in the knowledge that I can depend on your friendship, I need the strength and boost of confidence and happiness that your love and prayers will bring to me. Thank you.

Mary

My love,

Alláh'u'Abhá.

Forgive me for addressing you so but I cannot restrain myself. Words, like a whirlwind of worlds, leave me lost. I am a rat in a maze, confused – moving, but without pattern or design. The one whose words I long to hear is silent.

Writing is such a poor expression of love. My letters are romantic, inspired, willful – these things are all a part of love and a part of me; but when they are confined to scratches on a piece of paper they can't express me and they can't express love.

When I pray, I cannot pray, but only cry. Beyond words . . . beyond sounds . . . are only tears and contortions of the soul. Please forgive me. I beg God to forgive me for being who I am; I beg God to recreate me to be who He will have me be.

I love you and you love me.

164

'Each was aggravating to the other'

(The union of irreconcilables, after an ancient Hindu painting. Courtesy of Niedeck Linder, Zurich)

And I love you again; if you cannot return this love, then allow a
poet his passion and his pain. I would ask no more. I can be no less.

My love, Adam

Dear Adam,

I just received your letter today. Are you so full of grief? Why,
precious sensitive heart? But you are a Bahá'í! You are progressing
as a creature of God, you are teaching, you are deepening yourself.
Beloved one with the beautiful smile, God will take away all your
inner conflicts – you will become a new being – full of confidence,
no more self-doubts – just be a little patient with yourself.

But why not be happy while you wait? Work patiently for the
transformation. Why not be joyful?

You are full of love – just love, desire nothing but to obey God's
commands. He wants you to be joyful. How else can you show you
have the greatest news – let it show in your beautiful smile. Let
nothing sadden you – all in life is meaningless. Sweet one, just enjoy
yourself. All in creation was made for you to enjoy so that you
would be truly thankful.

You will pioneer – don't worry – it's already all planned out for
you. Just trust God and enjoy yourself now. Please be happy – there
is no reason to be sad. We know the blindness and depravity of the
world – we dwell with God in the world to come – we dwell there
now – our only desire is to worship God in a happy way, serve Him
happily for oh, how high a station is service to Bahá'u'lláh.

Yes, you will find a devoted wife – you will have a bosom friend, a
best friend – yet we still go through life mostly alone. Between God
and ourselves is where our happiness lies.

We humans have a habit of seeing the bad in ourselves, our
current occupation and activities. Now as the devoted Bahá'í that
you are – you stop it. There's a world of good, beautiful, marvelous
things within you – God dwells on His Throne.

So let your heart sing with joy as supremely as a sensitive Bahá'í's
heart can. Rise above all that immediately faces you – none of it
matters – just worship and serve your Beloved.

Everything you need and desire is known and will be given to you
– so let go of your sadness, my sweet. I love you and many others
love you – the next world loves you. Allow only positive thoughts
to enter your consciousness and allow only love to exude from your
being – be a guiding light, a lamp, a dew to the soil of the heart!

My sorrow was deep the year before I left for Sarawak. Only because I was in the habit of dwelling on the negative, because of lack of confidence in myself. Now see me – living proof – I have all that I desire – a teaching job, a good place to live, people to be with and laugh with, money to provide for myself, a pioneer post, and every day that passes is a happier day because it is one more day at my post. I pray to God that He will allow me to remain here – as it is the desire of the Guardian.

I could be sad about not losing the weight I want to lose, not learning the language fast enough, not having a close friend – but I'm so thankful to have a job that is a service – a room of my own – people to laugh with – so thankful to see that I am gaining in confidence, that the negative things are not very real to me – it is pleasurable for me to dwell in only a positive world – I like it.

Supreme confidence is something Bahá'ís should have to dispel all doubts.

I love you. I hope this letter makes your heart fly with happiness as it does so beautifully and easily. Write again soon and tell me how you are.

Mary

Everything you desire and more will come to you when the time is right. (I am in the right time and so thankfully happy.)

My Beautiful Mary,
   Alláh'u'Abhá.
You are the joy of my heart, and the sun during a spring shower. Your touch is the warmth of love coaxing blossoms and fruits from a tree dormant with winter; but you must not speak so much about me in your letters – speak about you. I want to know you. I want to love you.

Do not believe that I am unhappy. Deep within my heart is a happiness too deep-rooted to ever be displaced. It is roused to its plenitude by the eyes of a friend, the smile of a little girl, or the comforting words of a loved one. What you mistake for unhappiness is the agony that accompanies love; my grief is the expression of the knowledge of my separation. My lack of self-discipline brings about a separation from the reality that I am: this finds expression in regret. My separation from you and from those I love finds expression in a sadness of almost unscaleable height. My separation from the Beloved of all creation destroys and recreates

167

me: it is the writhing and the tears that accompany death and birth. It is a manifestation of the words:

> 'Thou seest, O my God, how my tears prevent me from
> remembering Thee and extolling Thy virtues, O Thou
> the Lord of the Throne on high and of earth below:'

I love you. And I must believe, as foolish and arrogant and self-deceiving as it must seem to you, that one day we will marry. And I further believe – in opposition to what you voiced in one of your letters – that the heart is not uncontrolled and un-understandable; instead it is susceptible and guided by the spirit, and known of the soul. It is the seat of His descent, and I bear witness that I have been created to know Him.

I have changed schools. In August I will leave for Tanzania. I will stop in London, in Haifa and in Cairo. My next letter will not be from California – may God bless this land of green trees and gray skies – but from a place of greater service. Please send your letters to my mother's for the time being – she will forward them. Because of this, I will probably write before I have received a response – a most dangerous proposition: the last time I did that you decided not to marry me! But such risks only exist to be taken. My prayers are for you and for Sarawak.

My love, Adam

This is the last letter; with it Mary seems to vanish. Adam said that she stopped writing. I suspect, however, that some of his early poems were written for her. Some few of his 'Tanzanian Poems' appear in the next chapter; the love poems are not among them. They were mostly of that quality that must be written but should not be published. Thus we shall have to leave Mary in the mist into which she vanishes and go on with Adam.

4

Mary had written that Adam had neither money nor a college education. This was true, but it was also true that he didn't particularly want them. He was a dreamer in a world without dreams, a prophet in search of a message, a hero in exile.

'If it pleases her,' he thought, 'I might as well return to the schooling system. I am miserable anyway – what can one more unhappiness do?'

But, lest the insane should lose his hard-earned sanity altogether, he also bought a motorcycle. It was the embodiment of wind and rain, dirt and crushing cold; it was a moment of glorious freedom. And typical of the way Adam did things, having bought the motorcycle he could not afford the gasoline to run it; this was often his only source of laughter. (Once, a few years before in Las Cruces, Adam had saved his money and bought a fine pair of steel-toed, steel-shanked, leather work boots; but after doing so he didn't have the money for socks so the boots sat beside his bed for a month while he laughed at himself.)

The university was as bad as Adam knew it would be. It was all too easy. There was no challenge, no learning, and very few people with intelligent or bright eyes. By his second term he was forced to take action: he had not really begun to study, so he couldn't stop. He carried his next twenty-one credit hours sitting on the bank of a river with his feet in the water. Even that was frustrating so he went to Canada for a few weeks. The system never even knew he was gone.

It was the system that so frustrated Adam. The system was blind, deaf, dumb, and if a person didn't realize it, the system's fat feet would trample him. America had changed. It was not the America Jefferson had envisioned or even the America Lincoln had fought for. It was a new creature entirely, and it was ugly. In many ways it had become one of the creatures of revelation that the prophets reveled in describing: the kind with steel feet, an iron belly, grasping hands, and a dozen horrible heads but no eyes. The founding fathers had tried to take many things into account and to make provision for them, but I suppose they could not have imagined that industrialists would grow so greedy, so many bureaucrats grow so blind and uncaring, and so many of the people grow so innocent and submissive. But that is what happened. In a letter to a friend, Adam guessed that wealth had gone to America's head like a gambling fever. He wrote that it was 'the New Deal that dealt it and the Great Society that played the house. The deck has been stacked! The damnable thing is that you can't tell the people who play the cards because they think they're winning. They don't know what winning really is. And the educational system is the heart of the whole mess . . .' This caused two things to happen to Adam. First, he grew to despise all the more—from his belly to his brain—the way we train our children. Second, it confirmed in him the desire to become a true educator.

Then the house fell in. America showed her true colors. It was the Persian question that brought them to the fore. There was the revolution in Iran and the staff of the American Embassy were taken hostage. That was a backward act at best, but America's reaction was even worse. Americans beat up Iranians, broke the windows of their houses, and ransacked their businesses. A wave of hatred and prejudice directed against anyone of Mediterranean complexion swept the country. That was enough for Adam; he couldn't live in this America any longer. There is a slogan about America: 'Love it or leave it', and when this slogan was directed against him twice in a single day, he decided to follow its advice. He would leave America.

He walked into the Foreign Students' Office one Monday morning and asked if they had any information about schools that could offer him the opportunity to study in Africa. The receptionist reached for a file on one of the shelves, opened it and handed it to Adam. He sat down in a chair and began to read the entries. The fourth or fifth page was a circular from Friends World College in Huntington, New York. After a resume of some very fine ideals, it listed programs it had around the world. East Africa and India were among the places mentioned – both were places that Adam had always wanted to visit. He took the address and wrote for application papers. Six months later he was enrolled as a full-time student on a project in Tanzania.

CHAPTER IV

*Being the story of Adam's pilgrimage, of Tanzania
and his first poetry, and of his restless romanticism*

And Israel beheld Joseph's sons, and said, Who are these? And
Joseph said unto his father, They are my sons, whom God hath
given me in this place. And he said, Bring them, I pray thee, unto
me, and I will bless them. Now the eyes of Israel were dim for age,
so that he could not see. And he brought them near unto him; and
he kissed them, and embraced them. And Israel said unto Joseph, I
had not thought to see thy face: and, lo, God hath shewed me also
thy seed. And Joseph brought them out from between his knees,
and he bowed himself with his face to the earth . . . And he blessed
Joseph, and said, God, before whom my fathers Abraham and Isaac
did walk, the God which fed me all my life long unto this day, the
Angel which redeemed me from all evil, bless the lads; and let my
name be named on them, and the name of my fathers Abraham and
Isaac; and let them grow into a multitude in the midst of the earth
. . . In thee shall Israel bless, saying, God make thee as Ephraim and
as Manasseh: and he set Ephraim before Manasseh. And Israel said
unto Joseph, Behold, I die: but God shall be with you, and bring
you again unto the land of your fathers.

Genesis 48:8–21

I

Love, though a harrowing experience, is perhaps the greatest
chastener known to the soul of man. A soul in love never rests; what
rest can there be when far from the Beloved? It is forever chased
down alleyways dank with the shadows of fear and expectation.
This must be so because love will not abide either of these strangers
in the heart it has chosen as home.

His breast is void of patience and his heart hath no peace.
A myriad lives he would forsake to hasten to the abode of
his beloved.*

* Bahá'u'lláh, *The Hidden Words*; from the Persian, number 4.

Adam had managed to get his loves all confused. If he were asked whom he loved, he would reply that he loved God alone. But then, if it was said that he acted as though he were pining after a woman, his heart would become silent and his eyes grow moist. That year was a heart-rending time. Letters from Mary were terrible: she was kind, but there is no kindness for the lover save deliverance. Then, during the month of Fasting, with a thousand unrelieved and throbbing burdens upon his heart, his visions began.

They formed themselves first in the pools of his tears and in dawn's eastern horizon. Then they grew in scope, dimension and color in his prayers. Let him begin to pray, but as soon as his forehead touched the ground words and sounds blurred in the flood of images that centered around the Qiblih in 'Akká and again around the destroyed house of the Báb in Shíráz. At each he followed a path to the Holy Place, ascended the stairway (of the House in Shíráz) and drew close to the seat of sanctity. He would prostrate himself on the ground and there offer his prayer. He could smell the flowers, touch the carpets, and see the lighted lamps. When the prayer was finished he would awake and find the muscles in his lower legs and thighs buzzing from improper circulation. He had no idea how long he had been prostrate on the ground. He knew only that it was not long enough. He had to go to Israel. He could no longer stay where he was.

There was yet a twinge of fear in his heart until one morning when he awoke to the songs of the morning birds. The rising sun was pouring a golden stream of assurance over his waking eyes and it melted his fears of growing and changing and leaving the old behind. They melted and dripped like thick molasses onto the floor and were swept out of his room, through the crack beneath the door, by the golden flood of morning sun. His soul changed and he entered a wide new realm.

In the mail that same day Adam received a letter of acceptance from Friends World College. He was to attend a brief orientation in New York at the end of July, then fly to London for two months of seminars in the techniques, philosophies and profession of creative writing. From there, if he wished (and he did), he could arrange an independent tour of research and writing in East Africa. It was as though the world opened its doors to his feverish knock on that day. His sadness melted into a joy that knew no bounds. London, it was true, he could do without, but even in that city he was sure to learn

many things. Awaiting him after that brief period would be Africa's
Rift Valley and the lake regions of which he had dreamed since he
was a child. And, best of all, he was free to arrange a short trip to the
Holy Land on his way to Africa.

God be praised! The world was bright again and the birds sang in
a summertime chorus. The sun, now released from the dark clouds
that limited it and hid its light, shed its glory in loving measure over
all creatures; Adam no longer felt bereft of these blessings.

The classes in London were good; very good, but because Adam
made them so. He wanted to write and to write well. He wanted to
teach people through writing, he wanted to learn much more of
himself through writing. However, even with this strong urge
within him, his heart was seldom in the bleak city streets of London.
It was in 'Akká, Israel.

When the period in London was completed Adam hurried away.
He hitch-hiked through the rains of Germany, the traditional quiet
of Austria, the mountains of Yugoslavia, and the history of Greece.
He lingered for a day or two where the mountains touched the
morning sun, where plums were ripe to be picked, or where the
Gods were said to dwell in the misty highland passages. But when he
came to the Aegean Sea his heart could linger no longer over passing
wonders. On the other side of that brilliant aqua ocean he knew the
waves lapped against a fortress wall and its sea gate rang with the
echo of the words: 'Upon Our arrival We were welcomed with
banners of light, whereupon the Voice of the Spirit cried out saying:
"Soon will all that dwell on earth be enlisted under these banners."'
Bahá'u'lláh's actual entry was heralded by the jeers and taunts of an
ignorant and fanatical population and He and His family waded
through a sea that spewed garbage and rot upon the shores.

Adam hesitated: he was very close to his dream. What if it were
not as he envisioned it? What if he, himself, were not ready? He had
turned down an opportunity to visit this Land earlier – while yet in
France – knowing then that he was not ready. Was he ready now?
He didn't know. There were many stories – too many stories; they
were culled into two kinds. The vast majority were of the
excitement, the exhilaration, the unparalleled joy of the pilgrimage;
but there were those few that frightened: stories of someone who
had gone on pilgrimage and returned only to leave the Faith, of
someone who had gone pioneering and had returned in absolute
despair. During the Fast just past, a friend had resigned from the

Faith after an initial visit to the House of Worship in Wilmette. Though they were separated by two thousand miles at the time, Adam knew the very moment that the decision was made and he whispered aloud, 'Paul, why do you leave me all alone?' But there was no answer save, perhaps, the question in the sea-wind now: 'Adam, are you ready?'

Adam chose to take the step chronologically. He thought that would help to prepare him; it didn't. He decided to go to Jerusalem first: to the musty, ill-fashioned burial places of David and the kings. He put on a skullcap as he entered, and, before he left, a sadness that one who could yearn after his God as David had should come to this. He went to the Dome of the Rock where Abraham was said to have offered Ishmael in obedience to the Will of God, and where Muhammad was said to have taken his Night Journey. Adam doffed his shoes in respect and prepared to enter. But he was stopped immediately by a guard who demanded that he purchase a ticket. Money! The man wanted money before he would allow Adam to enter a place sacred to all the world's people! Others were quite content to pay but Adam was disgusted. He turned around and walked away. He never did see the interior of the great golden dome.

He spent the next few days wandering through the old city and found it an amalgamation of peoples and cultures and histories. Jerusalem was a wonder, provided the visitor with a sensitive heart stayed clear of the Holy Places. But Adam tried again. He would not be accused of lacking perseverance in a thing so dear to him. He went to the Western Wall of the Temple and found young boys with earlocks waving and whispering like young trees in the wind. Beside them a soldier rocked a machine-gun cradled in his arms. Adam felt that the pigeons who made their homes in the wall and silently glided above the mourners were closer to God. Israel was not a religious state and it was not difficult to understand why! He went to the Church of the Holy Sepulcher but it must be said that he doubted from the moment he entered the gates. A story has it that a Muslim holds the key to the gates because no one of the Christian sects could be trusted not to lock all the others out. If the story is not true, it might as well be. The Church was a musty cavern with dozens of altars and caves (sanctified by the different sects) that celebrated the exploits of templars, priests, saints, martyrs and, by the way, Jesus of Nazareth too. Adam left after he watched a westerner (very probably an American) bow and kiss the slab of stone where Christ was supposed to have lain. The man was undoubtedly sincere in his worship, but Adam was repulsed by sincerity in the midst of such oppressive hypocrisy and confused disunity.

Adam turned north and traveled slowly to Haifa. He had much to get out of his mind, much dust to knock off his shoes. The excursion to Jerusalem showed religion in a very poor light. It was no wonder people turned away. What awaited him to the north? the last hope and refuge of a decaying civilization? the matrix and vortex of a new world order? He had already seen unnumbered proofs of it: proofs in himself and proofs in others. What the cities by the sea represented had already been the cause of an unchallengeable and undeniable growth within him. He did not doubt, but he did wish he had never gone to Jerusalem.

Adam had only three nights in the Haifa-'Akká vicinity and therefore every hour was precious. He arrived early in the morning and immediately secured a bed in a hostel at the foot of Mount Carmel. He washed and put on his suit. In Jerusalem also he had put on shirt and tie but had soon found them entirely out of place. He ascended the labyrinth of steps up the hillside. He could have taken a bus, but he somehow knew it was better to walk. The mid-morning sun had not yet become discouraging.

Haifa was a young city, light and airy when compared to Jerusalem. Its buildings were not particularly beautiful but the building stone, like the stone throughout Israel, was cut from the desert rock and had a distinctive and charming flavor about it. Adam entered the Persian Gardens and found them in total confusion. They were obviously beautiful, well designed and peaceful – usually. But just then they had been sporadically dug up for the placement of new water pipe. The birds emphatically disapproved of this digging. They chattered and bickered endlessly trying to decide what to do with the workmen. The workmen – most were Arabs native to the area – were all smiling. They made Adam smile too. It was utterly delightful: this confusion. As he walked along the occasionally uprooted garden paths he began to feel as though he were walking alone through a world being rebuilt. It was a good feeling, natural, and expressive of the state of the world and of the small band of Bahá'ís in it. He wondered how often Shoghi Effendi, who designed these gardens, had felt this way.

The Shrine of the Báb was undergoing repairs and so was closed, but that first time it was enough to circumambulate the beautiful monument. As he slowly circled the Shrine within the colonnade he prayed that he might be of service in Africa, and when each time he came to the northern side of the monument he gazed down the mountain side and across the bay. But what he searched for was lost in the morning mist.

He climbed to a quiet place beneath a ring of cypress and, as it was now the noon hour and the workmen had gone for the midday meal and *gailula* (siesta), there said his prayers. It was enough for one day. The Shrine of Bahá'u'lláh at Baḥjí was to re-open on the following day. He would be there; the rest of this day could be well spent resting and preparing himself for the morrow. His mind and spirit were already united and flowing. He had begun to feel as though he had come home.

Adam arrived at the Shrine at Baḥjí early on the following afternoon, and was immediately swept through the iron gates onto the path of crushed rock and tile by the exquisite beauty of the gardens. They were elegant and refined, and breathed a perfume of purity and unobtrusive sanctity. They were incomparable, except perhaps to that very rare and regal kind of woman . . .

He walked slowly – there was no need to hurry the moment – and watched the peacocks that guarded the doors to the chamber he had long dreamed of entering, slowly approach him. But the peacocks were of stone and it was a dream, the dream he had dreamed a hundred times and was now in the midst of again. But it was different this time: it was fuller, lighter, more brilliant; the cypress were far more majestic than he could have imagined and the flowers filled the air with an inebriating perfume that he knew would linger in the recesses of his mind for days to come. He entered the great carved doors and walked silently to the Sacred Threshold. He never took his eyes off the carpet. He bowed and kissed the step as he had done a thousand times before, then he rose again and repeated the Prayer of Visitation. Again he drew near and rested his mind and his heart on the threshold and on the carpets. He was alone and for two hours nothing stirred within or without the Shrine save the wings of his prayers, and no sound was heard but the call of the bird of his heart.

I testify that Thou hast been sanctified above all
attributes and holy above all names. No God is there but
Thee, the Most Exalted, the All-Glorious.*

He arose to leave as evening fell but returned the following day.
When he slowly walked the path to the iron gate, leaving for the last
time, he prayed that his services in Tanzania would be accepted and
that thereby he might earn his way back to the garden again. It is said
that the first visit is a gift but that the second must be earned.

2

The year Adam spent in Africa was a successful and profitable one
on the whole. There were troubled times and hurdles to master but
things always worked out for the best. When he had to explain why
he was in Tanzania he would give either of two seemingly different
reasons: he was there because the region had fascinated him since he
was a child and now he had come to experience and reflect it in his
writing; he was also there because he was a Bahá'í, and being there,
an American among Africans, teaching and serving side by side in
the ranks of a world-unifying cause, brought his faith and his work
together into a more complete whole.

His writing was comparatively prolific that year. He made it the
visible proof of his self-discipline. When the year was out he had
amassed three medium-sized volumes of work. He had kept a daily
journal, had written a series of essays on different aspects of the
problem of education in Tanzania, and had written a small
collection of poems and short stories.

Rather than trying to describe Adam's adventures and growth in
Tanzania for you, I have let him do it himself through his journals
and his poems. He made them available to me and here are some
severely edited passages.

*From the Journals: The text of a talk given to the Namangetti
Women's Literacy Class:*

... After an introduction where I was told and repeated each
woman's name (much to the delight of all), I began.

'It is normal and expected that children be in school and be
learning their reading, writing and maths. But it is a wonderful thing

* From the Long Obligatory Prayer revealed by Bahá'u'lláh.

when the adults are also in the classroom learning these things. It is a sign that Tanzania is strong and has a wonderful future. It makes me especially happy to see so many women learning because you, the women, are the first teachers of the children, and if the children are to be educated, then you, the mothers, must be educated. Bahá'u'lláh, Whom Bahá'ís believe to be the Messenger of God for this new age, said time and time again how very important it was that the women be educated. He even said that if a family has a boy and a girl and only enough money to educate one of them, then they must educate the girl because one day she will be a woman and a mother and will have to teach her own children.

'In addition to the reading, the writing and the maths that you are learning, there is another kind of education, an even more important education, which you must have: spiritual education. God has sent us many Divine Teachers to give us this education. He sent us Abraham Who taught us the ways of God, and He was like a Standard I teacher. He sent us Moses to teach us the laws of God after we had grown and learned from Abraham, and Moses was like a Standard II teacher. When we needed a Standard III teacher God sent us Jesus Who taught us to love our neighbors as our brothers. Muhammad was like our Standard IV teacher and He taught us to submit to the Will of God. And today we have grown and developed and we need a new teacher for Standard V; today God has sent us Bahá'u'lláh to teach us world unity.

'Today we must accept all of our Teachers and learn from them all and not argue about which Teacher was better. God has sent them all to us. This is why today it makes me happy to see all of you learning to read and write. Because now you will be able to read the Holy Scriptures for yourselves and will be able to know the truth with your own hearts and minds, and will not have to depend upon the stories and opinions of others.

'So again I encourage you to learn well; strive to improve your lives; and struggle to know the truth . . .'

Here the pressures of time are first eclipsed and then washed away entirely by a song.

. . . We arrived at 10:00 a.m. and waited a good hour and a half before any but the Kimangetti believers began to straggle in. Apparently this waiting is a social norm; but for an American, born and raised on a time standard, it proves rather disheartening. With precious moments of daylight eluding our grasp, I began squirming in my chair and the Kimangetti community, fearing I might leave, called their children together to sing for me. It was beautiful; the purity and innocence of their spirit and the lovely sounds of their voices must have attracted the hearts of those from Teresia and Machemo for they came soon after . . .

Here are examples and comments on African hospitality. The third extract is Adam's record of a bout with malaria.

. . . In Onlero we spoke with John Sasaka who agreed to begin the Bahá'í children's classes in two weeks, and who was only unhappy that we could not stay as his guests for a longer time. It is a local belief, I am told, that a visitor is a gift from God and his stay should be lengthened as long as possible. If a visitor should leave before having chai or dinner it is as if that home has denied a gift from God . . .

. . . My experience (during this past week) has shown that repeated prodding and a strong initiative on the part of the traveling teacher is a necessity if he is going to be allowed complete and unrestrained use of his time and energies. This situation arises, it seems, because the traveler is a guest and is not expected to perform any exertion. The concept of 'being the servant of another' (so well developed here) needs to be expanded into a concept of 'our being servants, together, in service of this Cause' . . .

Sunday
(written on Tuesday)

. . . A fever came upon me during the night; I felt weak, tired and cold during the day, and remember that the normally over-bearing sun felt very pleasant in the early afternoon when I got out of bed to deliver my talk at the Women's Conference. I returned to bed as soon as the visitors had left.

At night I was cold and wrapped in four shirts and a blanket when Jotham, Sellah, Silva and one of the visitors to the conference who lived too far away to return home that same day, came into the room and began to exorcise the fever out of me. In very loud voices, ringing under the tin roof, they sang Bahá'í songs, demanded in their language that the fever leave – declaring that I was a visitor and had many more things to do, then stamped their feet and exhaled great breaths (apparently to frighten the fever), and said Bahá'í

179

prayers. Then the process began again. The second time around I had water thrown on me, and my chest and back rubbed with Sloan's Ointment, but by this time I had a resounding headache (when I become ill I am very sensitive to sound), and, though I appreciated their concern, I prayed God that they would soon finish; and too, I thanked God that I am not a Roman Catholic and will not have to undergo Last Rites on my deathbed.

Monday

. . . I remember having a series of strange dreams involving situations from which I could not extricate myself of my own will and would fall back exhausted letting fate untangle the situations. And I remember wanting to strangle a hen who came into the house and cackled continuously – but I didn't have sufficient strength to get out of bed.

I was in a state of delirium all day such as would crown a good Dostoyevsky novel. It led to some interesting insights, one of which I will mention here. Delirium, so I am led to believe, is a state of complete consciousness wherein one seemingly has control of his actions, but when they are examined in retrospect (their being pointed out by people shaking their heads at you), you begin to realize that you have much less control than you previously assumed. Fate or chance seems to play a large role in your moment-to-moment actions. Your conscious choice of reaction is off balance because the perception of external events is distorted . . .

The fever broke in the middle of the night – as quickly as it had begun.

Tuesday

I am still very tired but am noticeably improving. I have a slight headache and a severe pain where I was given the injection of quinine. I have spent today restlessly – alternately resting and writing . . .

. . . This is a good opportunity to give proper recognition to Stephen Lutunda. With no real notice he dropped his normal duties and guided me around his sub-location for a full week. He interpreted on every occasion and eased my path in many ways. And whether it was the Kinsindi language or Stephen I'm not sure, but everything that was translated to me came with the tone and balance of proverbs. The most commonplace idea seemed to take on the ring of eternity springing from founts of wisdom. I have a faint suspicion that the things that I said were translated in a similar vein . . .

Here is a stranger in Paradise:

. . . A stranger is always well watched and constantly observed: children are very open in this, and the adults are not less interested, only more circumspect in their observing. My speech is different, my ways are different, my air is different, and if I stop and stand in one place for a few minutes I am soon surrounded by tens of eager-eyed babies. Even among the Bahá'ís I am closely observed and my habits and inclinations are often taken as exemplary – therefore I must be very careful. For example, few of the Tanzanian Bahá'ís use the long obligatory prayer though it is translated into Kiswahili (this is not their mother tongue, simply a more prevalent foreign tongue), and thus when I find a quiet place and spend a half-hour whispering and completing a complicated pattern of genuflections I am closely observed. It is my hope that this example finds fertile ground, particularly in the hearts and minds of the children who are becoming quite proficient in both English and Kiswahili . . .

Paradise has its sordid side also.

. . . and all five of the others who chose to visit communities in West Lugulu and begin children's classes failed to do as they had said they would. Three of them accomplished between a third and a half of their portion, two did nothing, and one of those spent the four shillings which I had given him for transportation. I delivered two very heated lectures about Bahá'ís keeping their word: that if a person says that he will do a thing and then does not, he has, in effect, lied; and he will never be fully trusted again. From the one who took the four shillings I demanded its immediate return so that he would not be branded a thief. He left his house to look for the money, perhaps hoping I would leave, but I waited in his home for three hours, refusing to accept the required amount from his father, refusing the entreaties of the others with me that we leave, and finally after speaking with his mother, saying that her son was acting a fool by keeping a person waiting in his house for money that was due him, and that she should have pity on him and bring him back again, he returned and gave me the four shillings. I then told him that he must deeply consider what he had done, that he never again commit himself to something which he would not fulfill . . .

The final impression that these journals leave is one of men of two very different cultures, brothers, working and building together, today, but with tomorrow very much in their minds.

. . . I have the nagging fear that this journal is becoming repetitive. I know my days are. I have a presentation which lasts an hour or two but I have repeated it over one hundred times; although the goal is a necessary and important one and the words I speak are strong, encouraging, and inspiring, for me they have become tiring and not inspiring at all – I have heard them so many times. It takes a great patience and all my reserve strength to speak these words with the love that gives them effect. I realize as I write this that I need a day just to rest and regenerate the energy sufficient to let flow again. I have taken to carrying a photograph of 'Abdu'l-Bahá with me during the day and whenever the opportunity to sit in silence for a few moments presents itself I feast upon the strength and wisdom that radiates from that face. In these moments of exhausted reflection the inner weight and meaning of certain stories of 'Abdu'l-Bahá, which passed me by before, suddenly become apparent . . .

. . . I still believe the workload is misproportioned between the men and the women, but I have come to realize that it is not as far out of balance as I had at first thought. And in sincere Bahá'í families a balance is more readily found. As I am now working with specific individuals for a sustained period of time I begin to see the work that they (as men) must do, and the work that they must give up to do the tasks which I am having them do. I have a bird's eye view of the daily problems they face and the situation they must overcome.

At this time of the year all the men have plowing to do, and I have seen them rise at five a.m. to plow for three hours so that they can be free to visit the Bahá'í communities for the remainder of the day; there are food shortages and yet they accommodate a visitor (myself) in a style they themselves cannot afford; the winds at this time of the year can be very strong and I have seen the thatch roofing severely damaged: a special grass needs to be collected and the mending done – and I ask them to travel to outlying areas all day long; one of those helping me had not completed the payment of his bride-price and his wife's brother came to take the woman and her child back to her father unless the account were settled immediately – and there were no cows to give. These are the problems that they face daily. Yet all these men who are helping me to complete this project are doing the very best they can and they are succeeding . . .

I only wish I could also share with you the photographs which accompany his journals because each one of them tells a story in itself. Adam used his camera to good effect until one day when he was carrying both the camera and some sugar to a friend's family (sugar was in very short supply in that part of the country at that time – it was worth any trouble wherever it was found) in the same bag and the sugar spilled. His camera stopped working. Adam showed his philosophical bent and acquiesced in the realization that sometimes sacrifices must be made; they all enjoyed tea with sugar after many days of tea without.

Here are some of his 'Tanzanian Poems'. He begins the small collection with the following thought on the art of writing:

. . . Ten years ago I believed that the philosopher's path was the high road. But a long time since, I realized that it was not that at all; I found it a lowly path and base, and forever stopping short of the promised city.

And so it is, from time to time, that I can only think of the tools, pen and paper, with disdain and repugnance. The act of writing, at these times, produces only aversion and fear. Aversion of the lowly and less-than-I-am, and fear that I am succumbing to this unworthy activity only because I haven't the endurance for daily selfless service or the faith to envision daily service as the eternal and the true . . .

Consultation
– instructions to my child

An idea
is a balloon
tied
to time and place
like the sun to Andes' heights;
And man
is a breeze
tugging,
nudging,
carelessly guiding,
then passing free.

First Rains

Will every artist see!
For to every eye revealed
Is perfect artistry
In a thousand silver slivers
Piercing a mountain canvas
At evening sunburst.
O Fashioner! Forgiver!
Deliverer! – of rain
That touches children's tongues,
You soothe dry eyes
And sting uplifted palms.
Praise! The maize will thrive
And joy will tumble down
The steep inclines
And roar across the valleys.
And the mountain gold
Will yield to tender green again.

A Dawn Awakening

I arise from my slumber at the prick
Of her pinions; that black regret is past;
Dawn has spread her wings and taken flight.
She rides higher, circling,
Surveying her dominions:
Her sharp sight lights on every cranny,
And is cast about every back egress.
In a moment she sees me. I watch her
Through the swing of the branches,
The roll of the leaves
Of 'my powerlessness and Thy might'
– the words being mine;
The last secret soul of me.

When It's Over

What with capitalists and communists
the whole damn world has gone to the economists
and they'll blow it straight to hell!
The bloated, grotesque earth will belch and swell;
our madness will climax,
crescendo, crash
in the rolling,
splintering mass
of flesh-directed
minds.
Death or life
will all be one;
our madness
will have come
and gone
and we'll be free to see ourselves again.

That grasping, laughing death is at my heart's door!
    The night will not shelter me –
    I, who am my enemy.

A flat, yellow moon climbs over a wasted shore
    Reflecting me, disdainfully,
    As Venus Panderer flees.

My breast is torn open by the Dark God's wild boar;
    My night dog stares pitilessly,
    My eyes ache in watching me.

Breathing-sweet and fly-infested, ever wanting more;
    But night will not envelop me,
    I am of the Burning Tree,
    I alone can set me free.

3

When Adam was twelve years old there had been a BBC broadcast on the television. For two hours each Wednesday evening for two months Adam (and his father) sat glued to the screen as the story of Sir Richard Francis Burton's first expedition into East Africa in search of the legendary Mountains of the Moon and the headwaters of the Nile was re-enacted before them. When the program was finished Adam went to the local library and found a thick biography of Burton. His heart had been caught and a life-long fascination with that era and that region had been kindled. This was a major reason why he was in Tanzania and working in the villages that hugged Lake Victoria.

No sooner was his project completed than the romantic restlessness that had prodded him all his life began again. As he watched two hippopotami lumber onto the bank after their bath on an evening in June, it occurred to him that he could not be this close to one of the greatest rivers in the world and not travel its length. It would be sacrilegious! There could be no consideration of revolutions or famines – the air was always ripe with the rumor of such things. And, after all, India was his next destination and the river was on the way, kind of. But, most assuredly, it was on the way back to the Holy Land.

'The romantic restlessness that had prodded him all his life began again'

(From The Waite Tarot Cards; Rider and Co. Ltd.)

He packed his books, his papers, and his typewriter and posted them to a friend in India. He arranged his visas. He packed one change of clothes, a blanket which he would give away before the trip was over, a mosquito net and his pipe and tobacco. He put these into a canvas shoulder-bag; it weighed just five kilos. Then he set off.

It was a wonderful trip. For three months he let the wanderlust guide him (he had no choice – he had forgotten to pack a map). He rode on the top of canvas-covered lorries over roads that weren't roads at all but tire tracks on an ancient commercial route; he rode mules, and a camel on one occasion for a short distance; he took the Nile steamer from Juba to Korti; the train that went no faster than a fast walk across the Nubian Desert; he took anything that moved. He crossed the Tanzanian-Ugandan border without problems because the Tanzanian troops were still in control and they liked his Kiswahili. He spent a few days in Kampala but the bullets buzzing around the city all night reminded him that it was the Nile he had come to see. The Bahá'ís who lived in that city were men with wives and young babies there to repair the Temple but who could not guarantee their families their next meal, an eighty-year-old woman from Germany who ran a kindergarten, sent the children home in the late afternoon, locked her doors and slept soundly in spite of the sporadic rifle fire that erupted throughout the night, and a number of others who were trying to rebuild an administration that had only recently been made legal once again. With a prayer for their continued perseverance he continued north to the Sudanese border. There he spent three days relaxing in the sun and three nights eating and haggling with the Police Commissioner because the gentleman liked his blanket and was suspicious of his English. Finally, after leaving the blanket behind, Adam was allowed to cross into the Sudan.

He waited for two weeks in Juba for the steamer to show up; 'it was expected any day'. He spent two weeks on its roof alternately cringing and shivering in the rains and stretched out with his pipe between his teeth listening to the water thrown from the ship's wake lap into the endless reeds of the Sudd. Then the slow train north out of Khartoum: it stopped all night long and three times each day for prayers. In the middle of a blistering desert the Muslims would pour out the doors and the windows hoping to get a good place on the sand. After the motions of washing, they would begin their prayer.

It was a beautiful scene, and Adam would often walk a short distance into the desert just to look back and capture it in all its breathtaking glory. There, in an endless ocean of sand where nothing broke the horizon save the jagged hills far to the northeast, was a small worm-like train curled on a track which disappeared in either direction into the distant, shimmering sands; of this Adam wrote:

Among the Believers

When the train stopped
They tumbled out the windows
Onto the Nubian sands.

There are no other creatures
For a thousand miles round;
Only these who murmur and bow
Before their God.

They have washed themselves in the sand,
Buried themselves in the sand;
And one wept.

No one will know that this day was;
Only the distant mountains
Will testify of their faith
When the train rolls on.

A month in Egyptian bazaars – enough to sour any soul – then across the UN peacekeeping zone and he was in Jerusalem again. But he was careful this time: though he walked through every bazaar and hidden alley of the old city, he did not enter any Holy Place. He prepared himself to go to 'Akká once again. He reflected over his year in Africa and brought it to culmination in his mind, concluding that he had learned two things during the year. Both were aspects of the concept of detachment and true affection. First he learned that it did not matter whether he lived in Africa, in India, or even in America. Wherever he lived he would be at home. Secondly, he learned that, true as it was that we should not love God for the blessings He bestows, yet the attributes of His own essence – wisdom and eloquence, power, courage, and perseverance – are given us that we may use them to serve, that they may flow through us as through a hollow reed to testify of God and not of us. When the opportunity to serve lapses then these attributes must return like the sun's rays do to the sun. Only then will all our days be lighted and bright. We must love God and obey his laws for love of His Beauty alone rather than in greed for His attributes.

Adam was ready to return to 'Akká.

CHAPTER V

Being how Adam's self-recrimination and guilt give fierce battle and are at last subdued by willed patience and ease. About God, and laughter, and happiness. And how Adam sees the child he is no more

And Jacob called unto his sons and said, Gather yourselves together, that I may tell you that which shall befall you in the last days . . .
Joseph is a fruitful bough,
Even a fruitful bough by a well;
Whose branches run over the wall:
The archers have sorely grieved him,
And shot at him, and hated him:
But his bow abode in strength,
And the arms of his hands were made strong
By the hands of the mighty God of Jacob;
(From thence is the shepherd, the stone of Israel:)
Even by the God of thy father, who shall help thee;
And by the Almighty, who shall bless thee
With blessings of heaven above,
Blessings of the deep that lieth under,
Blessings of the breasts, and of the womb:
The blessings of thy father
Have prevailed above the blessings of my progenitors
Unto the utmost bound of the everlasting hills:
They shall be on the head of Joseph,
And on the crown of him that was separate from his brethren.

Genesis 49:1, 22–26

I

The trouble began in earnest after Adam's three nights in Haifa. It had been building in Africa and had become particularly noticeable on the Nile excursion, then again in Jerusalem. The Bay of 'Akká had given his soul a short respite. Now, on that same shore but farther north, near the Lebanese border, it had begun again and it was worse. It was like the words of the song by Donovan: 'Happiness runs in a circular motion / Thought is like a little boat upon the sea / Everybody is a part of everything anyway / You can have everything if you let yourself be.' Adam was adrift in a very wide sea in happiness's little dinghy. For the person not in it, it must have looked very pleasant, very good fun indeed. But being on the inside looking out was a different experience altogether. The waves were building and every twirl and splash told Adam that there was a storm coming. Oh, a very big storm and he was beginning to feel seasick.

> Know ye from what heights your Lord, the All-Glorious is calling? Think ye that ye have recognized the Pen wherewith your Lord, the Lord of all names, command-eth you? Nay, by My life! Did ye but know it, ye would renounce the world, and hasten with your whole hearts to the presence of the Well-Beloved. Your spirits would be so transported by His Word as to throw into com-motion the Greater World – how much more this small and petty one!*

Adam, in his little dinghy, traveled across the Mediterranean to Athens, then again to Cairo, and finally to Bombay. The storm went with him; there was no escaping it. The waters became great troughs and he was thrown from their peaks to their depths to their peaks again with dizzying speed. But make no mistake about it, these were not the 'oceans of grandeur', rather it was a terrible storm of self-doubt, remorse, self-denunciation and self-recrimination.

Adam had always examined his own actions with daily scrutiny, but this was the process gone mad. The fire of self overcame him and it was his own actions that burned him through. Every foolish word, every action that raised eyebrows, came rushing back at him, and each one shouted an accusation as it pushed by, throwing him to the ground with the force of its passing. But what became almost unbearable was the remembrance of words he had written – things so intimately a part of himself given to others as playthings: they were his blunders, his stupidities, his foolish audacities etched into eternity as surely as if they had been carved into stone. *Samskara*

* Bahá'u'lláh, a passage from the *Kitáb-i-Aqdas*.

held a knife at his throat as he carried *Karma* to the funeral pyre.

He wandered about the cities of India visiting the Bahá'í schools in Panchgani, Ooti and Gwalior; outwardly he was calm: a veritable daytime Dr Jekyll. But let evening's curtain fall and the eyes be dimmed and there was his Mr Hyde come again. He would walk the night streets mumbling and cursing and praying all at once and all half-aloud. He waved his arms about, thrashing the demons in the air, and occasionally brought them down on his own head with such force that at any other time the blow would have knocked him flat. Sometimes, with his arms still in the air, he would meet another voyager on the path. He would try to calmly bring his arms back to his side as their eyes met in the night. Then he would wonder if the other had the eyes of the angel Uriel and if he could tell a devil at a distance of ten paces. And no sooner had they passed, then so would Adam's affected calm. He would rage at himself all the more violently for having been caught with his self-possession gone.

Later Adam would describe this time with a laugh saying, 'It was like shaving last week's beard with last month's razor blade. It was like being pulled painfully into a new morning's light.' The result of all this pain was like the calm after a storm: there was peace from horizon to horizon.

In letters to friends written immediately after this conversion and reorientation he describes his contentment and calm:

Dearest Stephanie,
    Alláh'u'Abhá.
A letter after a long time, but with little to say except that I love you and think of you often. I am content and have no wishes that will not be fulfilled, no regrets of things that were – but I could not have written this two weeks ago. Indeed, had I sent you any one of the numerous letters I wrote (but kept) you would have thought me in deep despair, or senseless, though I was neither; I was only under passing clouds, looking up.
So I send you this simple love letter (is any other kind really worth the postage?) and a poem reflecting the calm of my soul:

<blockquote>
The night is muted and gentle
To be touched
Like a woman
Wanting to be touched,
On the rooftop at night.
</blockquote>

There are no glaring necessities,
Nothing need be done
In the sweet-smelling
Tobacco haze
On the rooftop at night.

I can be alone –
There are no scowling faces
To encroach upon my sight –
In the curling panorama
Of the rooftop at night.

Or again in a letter to me:

. . . I began this letter speaking about decisions and I think I want to return to decisions for a while: I have made two or three lately and I want to try to explain them clearly.

The first decision was that I wanted to write. You may say that it has taken me an awfully long time to come to this point, but that's the process; it is now a full-fledged decision. I suppose that I finally arrived at it because of my life philosophies, and my life position and directions. As you know I have followed a path that is uniquely my own and have ignored all social acceptance and criticism for a time. I have followed, and continue to follow, my path, conscientiously, and without reservations about where it might ultimately lead; doing this, it now occurs to me that such honest and compassionate self-discovery is an alternate and highly rewarding path for all. It holds the possibility of more reasonable (even if more circuitous at first) and more stable growth. Therefore I feel the responsibility to learn to write well so that I can help present this alternative to people.

Deciding to write has, as a by-product, caused the drama of two other profound decisions. If you remember, I implied that all substantial decisions are both gradual and dramatic – it is the drama that occurred here. The first decision is one basic to the proper functioning of life but which, today, is more often shied away from or thought confining and to be escaped from. It is chastity. Thoreau called it the only virtue, and though it isn't quite that, it also isn't difficult to know what he means. Chastity is very much like honesty: it is very basic. I mean basic in the sense of something from which you build and without which you can't build solidly. It is also important that you know that I mean chastity and not celibacy.

Celibacy is rigid and cold – like mountain peaks. Chastity, on the other hand, is warm, light, dancing – like fire on the mountain tops. It has that ancient characteristic of signaling and guiding as fire on a mountain has. It is fluid like fire also: for example, chastity in marriage takes on the guise of fidelity.

Perhaps you will be interested if I describe how I came to this decision. I will tell of both the gradual and the dramatic. Much of the story you already know or have surmised but you should know it from my point of view. I will be brief (this letter is too long already).

Characteristically I approached it backwards. The episode began, I could say, some nine or ten years ago when it was necessary, because of peer pressure, to begin associating with girls with a more than carefree and playful purpose in mind. That expectation sent me into a tail-spin and a four-month-long depression. But finally, coming out of that and engaging the challenge as inevitable, I tackled it with all my strength and will. I might have been mercenary at times. However, all this is not to say I got very far – the American sexual scene at puberty is a maze that few ever find their way through. I was lucky. Some three or four years later – battle-scarred, at least psychologically – I re-emerged. I became a Bahá'í. And only found out after declaring myself that chastity was a law. The next scene, the explaining scene, with the lady I was seeing a lot of then, was heart-warming. But chiefly because she was a heart-warming character. I was lucky. Then came these last five or six years of playing around with chastity. It's a rather difficult thing to face straight on when you've allowed yourself to be conditioned backwards. My pet name for chastity, by the way, is 'that difficult virtue' – I think it fits. Anyway, one night over a year ago (as you know) I was feeling damn lonely and forgotten and I wrote a poem. I liked the experience and so began writing poetry more and more often, and eventually it was the poetry that led me to conscientiously, and as completely as I am now able to understand, assume chastity's protecting and empowering robe. Not so very long ago I became thoroughly disgusted with looking at this small collection of poems I had assembled. Most of them are bad and those that are not bad are not good enough. I can't tolerate inferior workmanship. You know that I often make unusual decisions and so it was with this. I did not decide to read and analyze more quality poetry (though I have since), I chose chastity. I needed more strength and a greater clarity of mind and chastity could offer these to me. It was the solution that, as I saw it, best fit the problem at hand, so I accepted it contentedly. With radiant acquiescence.

The second offspring of the decision to write is, perhaps, more characteristically defined as a revelation. It was the realization that I was content. Contentment, as you know, is soft, flowing, accepting and slow – like a stream through a meadow. It has the absolute awareness (harboring no doubt) that the quiet stream will eventually wind its way to the sea. A great satisfaction and self-confidence comes with contentedness. But this is not complacency or the inability to move and grow. Contentment is a rapture, it is all-absorbing, but it cannot be adequately explained except by the silent smile or a ringing laughter. It is sufficient to say, I think, that it is an exciting and significant change for one who has been tumbling down mountainsides and roaring through gullies for so long . . .

2

They were a small group that came together every Monday evening, only seven individuals, but sometimes it felt as if they lived only from Monday to Monday. They had already discussed some few of Bahá'u'lláh's other Tablets and for the last three weeks had been studying His Tablet to Aḥmad. Everything had been going smoothly until they came to the command:

> . . . Bear thou witness that verily He is God and there is
> no God but Him, the King, the Protector, the Incom-
> parable, the Omnipotent . . .

That's when someone said, "Who is God besides Whom there is no God but Him?' and when arguments, suppositions and theories began to fly through the air like lightning in the night sky.

A full hour later Cyrush leaned forward in his seat and declared, 'It doesn't matter whether we say that God is God (even though we're only going to have to explain that because it won't make much sense to many people) or Bahá'u'lláh is God or even Man is God. And it doesn't matter whether we say that Bahá'u'lláh sent the Báb or God sent the Báb or Who spoke on Sinai from the Burning Bush. The important thing is that we be selfless and clear-headed enough to say Bahá'u'lláh is God to the person who needs to hear that and Bahá'u'lláh is not God to the next person who needs to hear that. Both opinions are right and both are absolutely wrong. We are never going to be able to understand the mystery of this. The best we

196

are going to do is understand that we don't understand.' He said this in one long breath.

When he stopped to inhale Adam said, 'Lord, Cyrush, but you're a philosopher.'

Gita, Cyrush's wife, joined in, 'Yes, he is. Isn't he wonderful?' Then she turned to her husband, 'But, dear, I got lost halfway through,' and she laughed a full ringing laugh that was like light out of the East.

After a moment Adam rejoined, 'But our philosopher is right. What he said is exactly the same as an old argument in which I've locked horns with the priests and the nuns and the Sunday School teachers ever since I was this high.' He indicated with his hand above the floor that he wasn't very high at the time. 'They always had the answers but their answers weren't good enough. They believed that their little piece of Truth was the whole Truth, while I couldn't or wouldn't believe it. I guess that I have always felt that the difference between most of the people and the believers, between those who don't search and those who live to search, is that they believe that they already know, while some know that they are only coming to know.' Then he paused for a few seconds and looked at Gita, 'We can never come close to explaining God. And maybe the best that we can do is laugh; full and true, like you just did. After all, that's why the dervishes whirl in Omdurman on Friday afternoons.'

'Where is Omdurman only?' Raju asked, a little frustrated.

'Across the White Nile from Khartoum.'

'Oh! Adam, you are too confusing.'

'That, my friend, is because I am too confused!' Then he laughed also, and the others with him, like the dervishes do in Omdurman on Friday afternoons.

3

Adam laughed. The laughter welled up from nowhere – nothing seemed to have incited it – then it died again in the same way. It was like the old Chinese ideal of a traveler: he doesn't know where he's come from, and he doesn't know where he's going, he's just traveling.

'What's funny?' I asked.

'Oh!' Maybe he suddenly remembered I was there. 'Nothing . . . really . . . the world, I guess. It's a very funny world we live in.'

'It was like the old Chinese ideal of a traveler'

(Kuo Hsi, 'Early Spring'; Collection of the National Palace Museum, Taiwan, Republic of China)

We were traveling on a bus together returning from a day in one of the villages outside Lucknow. My son was sleeping on my lap; he was hot and tired and miserable. We had been in the bus for half an hour already and Adam hadn't said a word. I probably looked like I wanted a little more sociable company.

So he said, 'I suppose I'm not very good company. I get pretty quiet at times. I suppose there are two ways my happiness manifests itself. One is when I become silly and laugh and play like a child and tell foolish jokes that no one understands except me and so they can't really laugh at them. But it's okay because I enjoy the jokes so much that I laugh enough for everybody. People must think I'm a little bit crazy at those times and I suppose I am. The other way my happiness shows is when I become quiet, like today, and my mind drifts off into other worlds and then suddenly for no easily discernible reason the happiness just flows out of me in laughter. I really don't know what's funny. Maybe it's that somebody moved their head or hand in a way that tapped a memory which I can't even fully recall. I'm a fool; I guess I've always known that. But I'm sorry that I'm also such bad company at times.'

'Maybe you're not such a fool as you think. Or, maybe, there is wisdom in your foolishness. Perhaps you haven't noticed but when you're happy you have the gift of being able to make others happy and laughing also. It's a good thing because most of us are too self-conscious to be like that. Bahá'u'lláh writes somewhere – perhaps in the *Hidden Words*, it sounds like one of them – "Rejoice in the gladness of thine heart, that thou mayest be worthy to meet Me and to mirror forth My beauty." So you see, there is wisdom in your foolishness. You should never lose it.'

We continued talking about this and about a hundred other things. The two-hour trip to Lucknow was over before we knew it.

4

My son and I were sitting in the early afternoon sun in Lalbagh Park in Lucknow when Adam walked up. I had expected him an hour before and we had already begun to eat the Masala Dosa we had brought with us. 'You're just in time,' I said.

'That's funny; usually I'm late.' He was in a good mood.

My son gave him some Dosa wrapped in a crumbling brown leaf. 'Here. This one's for you.' John was seven years old, his hair was as blond as mine, and he was no more than four feet tall. But he thought he was pretty big. He had started school the year before and was now in the second standard. Also, he had already seen London, and Jerusalem, and he was now living in India. He and Adam got along fine because they were both world travelers. Sometimes they would sit and swap stories for an hour about the places they had been.

Adam burned his tongue on the chutney – I'd told him not to use so much – but he did it every time. He was worse than a kid. Then he turned to John and said, 'Must be a holiday; how come you're not in school?'

'Because it's a holiday. It's Ram's Birthday.'

'Oh. India sure has a lot of holidays.'

'Mom says that's because it's so old. I guess the older you get the more holidays you have.'

'That must be so. I know two real old men – they must be eighty-four years old – who have a holiday every day. They sit around playing checkers every day.'

'One day you'll be eighty-four too.'

'I hope so. So will you.'

'Not me; I'm gonna be one hundred and two. My great grandfather was one hundred and two.'

'In India?'

'Maybe. Who knows?'

'How come you're in India now?'

'You know.'

'Yeh, but I like you to tell me.'

'Cause my mother brought me. So that she could teach at Lady Doak College. Over there,' he replied pointing. We could just see the top of the chapel in the distance.

'Do you love your mother?'

'Sure do. Do you?'

'Shore 'nuf do.' John looked at me and smiled slyly.

'How come you talk funny sometimes?'

'Cause I like to.'

'Can you talk like an Indian? I can.'

'I like the way Indians talk.'

'So do I. But it sounds funny.'

'I'll bet they think you sound funny too.'

'They do. My friend Ravi told me so.'

'Do you like school or holidays better?'

'Holidays.'

'Me too. Why?'

'Because you can't talk in school.'

'But your mom likes school?'

'That's because she's a teacher and can talk all the time. Besides she's crazy.' Adam liked that and laughed. John ducked when I threw my water at him.

'What do you want to be when you grow up?'

'Everything.'

'Everything? Everything like what?'

'Everything like everything. I don't know.'

'Oh! You're a slow eater for someone who's going to be everything.'

'I'm finished.'

'I never would have known.'

'Let's play. Walk me around on your shoes like you did that other day.'

Adam heaved himself up off the ground but probably wouldn't have been able to do it without John's active encouragement. Soon they were facing each other, each holding the other's hands, and John on Adam's shoes. Every step that Adam took, John had to take too, but backwards. They walked around me twice like this when Adam asked, 'Where did you ever learn to walk like this?'

'You taught me. It's much better than walking in somebody's footprints.'

'I knew it must be better than something.'

'Where did *you* ever learn to walk like this?'

'I don't know. My daddy taught me, I guess.' Adam paused as if some thought had slowly crept up on him and then struck him. Then he said, 'I remember my dad would come home from work and as soon as he came in the door I'd run up to him and try to make him notice me. But he never would; he'd just keep on asking, "Where's Adam?" or "What's happened to that boy? I was expecting him to be at the door when I got home." No matter what I'd say to make him look down at me, he wouldn't take any notice. He'd say to my mom, "Trish, did you leave a teapot on the stove? I hear small noises like whistling or something." And my mom would say, "No, there's no teapot on." "Well, maybe there's a window open and it's the wind making those sounds. Now where could that son of yours have gotten to? Adam! Adam!" he'd call, and there I'd be pulling on his uniform. Then he'd say, "Trish, you must have left a window open somewhere. I can feel a breeze tugging and pulling at me." So I'd decide to stand on his feet and then it was as if I'd suddenly become visible and he'd say, "Well, there you are, boy. Where have you been? I was just about to go out and look for you." I'd say, "I've been here all the time. Didn't you see me?" "Nope, I didn't see hide nor hair of you. What are you doing there on my shoes? Move over a bit – that's my bad toe. You know I can't walk anywhere like this", and he'd walk me around just like we're walking now. Yep, that must have been how I learned to walk like this.'

'Your father sounds like he was a pretty good father, but couldn't he really see you?'

'I don't know. But I guess he was an okay father. Except that he never taught me to whistle or to blow bubbles with bubble gum. And I still can't do either of them. But he sure had big feet.'

'You have big feet too.'

Adam looked down at their feet and said, 'Well, maybe I do at that. I always used to ask my dad if I'd ever have feet as big as his. He'd look me in the eye and say, "We'll have to wait till you grow up, boy, and see." Then I'd tell him that I'd bet I'd have feet even bigger than his. He'd just say, "Maybe."'

'Are your feet bigger than his now?'

'They sure are.'

'You know, I can do both of them.'

'Both of what?'

'Whistle and blow bubbles with bubble gum. I'll teach you to whistle sometime if you want me to.'

'Okay. But let's sit down now. Your mama is probably getting lonely.'

As Adam and John sat down on the grass again, Adam turned to me and said, 'It doesn't seem like so very long ago that I was just as tall as John is now and was walking around on my dad's shoes. I guess I've finally grown up.'

EPILOGUE

Being Adam's epitaph

The words of the wise are as goads, and as nails fastened by the masters of assemblies, which are given from one shepherd. And further, by these, my son, be admonished: of making many books there is no end; and much study is a weariness of the flesh.

Let us hear the conclusion of the whole matter: Fear God, and keep his commandments: for this is the whole duty of man. For God shall bring every work into judgement, with every secret thing, whether it be good or whether it be evil.

Ecclesiastes 12:11–14

After returning to my home from the park that afternoon we cooked a simple dinner together. We finished eating, I took John off to bed and, on returning, as I approached the dining-room table, I could see that Adam had stacked all the dishes neatly on the end of the table opposite him. He had wiped the area clean, had found a pencil and paper and was busily scribbling away.

'What are you writing?' I asked as I drew near.

'Just a minute. Then I'll show you.'

I took the dishes into the kitchen and set them by the sink for the *ayah* to clean in the morning. I returned and sat down at the table again and waited.

When Adam had finished he looked up and smiled. Looking at the piece of paper again, he read it through to himself, stopping once to make some small correction. Then, still following the sheet, he began humming a tune that had been playing in his mind all afternoon. He looked up again and said, 'Do you remember that poet in Kerola – the one who wrote the poem "Banana" between bouts with a wine bottle?'

I nodded my head.

'Well, he also wrote his own epitaph before he turned over in some gutter for the last time. It was a beautiful conversation with the stars from beneath the slab of stone he knew they'd lay on top of him. I've always liked people who wrote their own epitaphs. There's something immortal about it. And here, just now, I was looking at your Sunday paper and there was a short article about one of the Mongol queens. Just a minute . . . what's her name? . . .' He reached for the paper and found the story: '. . . yes, Nur Jehan; she died in 1645. The night before she died she wrote this in her will: "On my grave be placed / Neither a candle nor a flower / That the lark and the moth / May be saved the agony of love." I'll bet it is in fine Persian verse too. Anyway, this prayer has been running through my mind for days and I think it makes a fine epitaph. Here, have a look at it and tell me what you think.' He handed me the paper on which he had been writing. It read:

He is God!
O my Beloved and my Desire!
Let my life be a chanted prayer
That will guide the hearts of children,
Gird the loins of youth,
And crown the hoar hairs of age.
Let my death be a sacrifice
To the generations to come.
Let the willow weep over my burial place,
But let no eye grow moist;
Let the children's laughter caress
The hillsides of the mount where I have died,
And let the wind sing
And the leaves dance to this song:

I believe in the future;
I believe in Tomorrow;
I believe in the children's laughter
And in their undimmed eyes.
I believe in the future,
I believe that the future is richer by far:
I believe in Tomorrow.
I believe in Tomorrow that tears won't flow:
I believe in the children's laughter.
And in their undimmed eyes:
I believe in the bright eyes of Tomorrow,
In the bright eyes of Tomorrow . . .